Alison Webster has been writing and editing on themes of theology and social transformation for more than twenty years. She is the author of numerous resource books that draw together social action and contemplation, most recently *Advent of the Real World: A Resource Publication for the Advent Season* (Oxford: Diocese of Oxford, 2006) and *Passion for Real Life: A Resource for Reflections in Holy Week* (Peterborough: Methodist Publishing House, 2007). Alison has a long-standing interest in identity issues, particularly gender, race, sexuality and disability, and is the author of *Found Wanting: Women, Christianity and Sexuality* (London: Cassell, 1995) and *Wellbeing* (London: SCM Press, 2002). She was a founder editor of the two international journals, *Theology and Sexuality* and *Political Theology*. Alison has worked for the Student Christian Movement, the Institute for the Study of Christianity and Sexuality and the Christian Socialist Movement. She now works as Social Responsibility Adviser for the Church of England Diocese of Oxford.

YOU ARE MINE

Reflections on who we are

Alison Webster

SPCK

First published in Great Britain in 2009

Society for Promoting Christian Knowledge
36 Causton Street
London SW1P 4ST

British Library Cataloguing-in-Publication Data

A catalogue record for this book is available from the British Library

ISBN 978–0–281–05935–5

1 3 5 7 9 10 8 6 4 2

Typeset by Kenneth Burnley, Wirral, Cheshire
Printed in Great Britain by Ashford Colour Press

Produced on paper from sustainable forests

Contents

Fear not, for I have redeemed you; I have called you by name, you are mine. When you pass through the waters I will be with you; and through the rivers, they shall not overwhelm you; when you walk through fire you shall not be burned, and the flame shall not consume you.

Isaiah 43.1–2

Preface and acknowledgements

One day, when I was in the middle of writing this book, my four-year-old niece began to tell me about a Disney film in which a frog wants to become a handsome prince. I asked her: 'Why do you think the frog wants to become a prince?' She simply laughed with incredulity and said, 'I really don't know. It's very silly. He is a frog.'

I was stopped in my tracks. Suddenly, I was made aware of my own assumption that to be a frog is a lesser fate than to be a prince. It seemed that my critical faculties had deserted me. Where was the self that should say, 'Hang on, why is it better to be a prince? Who says?' So a child's wisdom reunited me with a realization that if I am on a sinking boat in the middle of a lake, I'm better off as an amphibian than as a member of the royal family.

As well as being a shrewd one-sentence summary of the key message at the heart of this book, my niece's comment was also an empowering one in the context of the process of writing. Many who write will know the temptation to wish that one could write as a prince, when one is called to write as a frog (or vice versa) – the need to honour the style one has, and not wish it were otherwise; the need to speak the message that is given to you in the best way possible, and to wish to do no more than that.

It can be hard to hold on to this vision, and my heartfelt thanks go to all those who have shared with me their experiences of similar struggles, and who have therefore helped me to cling to enough self-confidence to continue when I might have given up: Jo Ind, Suzanne Keys, Rachel Freeth and Janice Price have all, in various ways, helped me to stay with the conviction that the intellect doesn't have to be separated from feelings, and that personal experience and poetry can be integrated with reason and rationality.

I extend my deepest thanks to the entire Okafor family for being siblings in creativity – while also offering insights and new perspectives at every juncture – not least in those innumerable dinner-time conversations, but also through who you are in the world, individually and collectively. Thank you, as ever, for all you are teaching me.

Thanks to others who read the text and offered comments along the way: those named elsewhere, and also Jane Winter, Ann Memmott and Ruth McCurry (my editor at SPCK). To Ruth I also owe a debt of gratitude for her faith in the project and her patience and flexibility over deadlines.

Writing this book has been a demanding spiritual process, one in which deep joy and pain have lived side by side and in sometimes erratic dialogue. My thanks go to Brian Thorne for his compassionate spiritual accompaniment and unnervingly accurate perceptions. Without him this book would quite simply not have been written. Thanks to Leslie Griffiths, my long-term and hugely respected mentor, for his passionate belief that I am not, and never have been, 'lost'. And to Ben Okafor, whose soul speaks to mine in ways that are mysterious and life-changing, and who hears my soul, even when I do not know that it is speaking – let alone what it is saying. Thanks to Ben for translating God back into a language in which I can communicate.

I thank my employers in the Diocese of Oxford for their immense encouragement and support and their manifest belief that my writing is part of my vocation. Rosemary Pearce, the Diocesan Secretary, and Martin Conway, Chair of the Board for Social Responsibility, have been unstinting in enabling me to invest time and energy in the writing process. My fellow Heads of Department, members of the Senior Staff of the Diocese, and colleagues in the Social Responsibility team have offered inspirational thoughts and ideas on the book's theme and have helped to shape what is found here.

Finally, inestimable thanks to Alex Wright for being a great partner and husband, for offering both confidence in my ability to complete the task, and reassurance that the book was realizable. As a fellow writer on issues of meaning and purpose, and as an accomplished publisher of religious books, his scepticism has kept me grounded, his humour has lifted me from despairing places, and his practical support and advice have helped me through to the project's end.

1

Questions of identity

——⟫•⟪——

'Consider the whole of history and prehistory – billions of years. Remember dinosaurs, ice ages, the evolution of humankind. Now project into the future. Imagine, if you can, a hundred years from now; a thousand; a million. Think about yourself. Here. Now. In all of that time past, there has never been another you. And in all of the time yet to come, however long our planet has left, there never will be again. There has been and will be only one of you on this earth – ever.'

I am back in school for a couple of days. The child being addressed is 11. His name is Glyn. His response to the teacher's message is like daybreak: a beaming smile and a ducking of the head in shy acknowledgement of his own specialness. A specialness shared, of course, by every other student in his class, and by each and every one of us.

Glyn's class has been exploring the notion of identity. They tackled this through a simple pen-and-paper exercise, a kind of word association game. The class was given a word: family. Working from this word, each child drew a 'linking' diagram with spaces for seven additional words. The aim was to write down the seven words which flowed from that one initial word, family.

After a few minutes, the teacher invited the children to share their last word.

'Goldfish,' said one.

Did any other child have 'goldfish' as their eighth word?

No. Of course not. Why not?

'Because our minds all work in different ways.'
And why is that?
'Because we have all had different experiences.'
Which means?
'We are all different.'

The teacher then asked one or two children to share all of their words: family-mum-dad-computer-games-fun-laughter-teeth; family-sun-stars-sky-plane-holiday-beach-donkey-straw; family-football-Everton-Manchester United-oranges-sponge-jam-cake. This simple exercise revealed the endless variation and diversity among just one class in one school in one town on one day.

I am suddenly struck by the radical simplicity of what this class has learned. And I am slightly disturbed by my surprise at the awe and wonder in Glyn's response. For it reveals to me that while Glyn inhabits his uniqueness, for the moment at least, as an astounding miracle, I live mine as merely axiomatic. I am no longer surprised or arrested by it. My intellect and common sense have appropriated it, torn it away from my heart and soul and evacuated its transformational potential.

What is this book about?

This book represents a passionate commitment to rediscover a lived awareness of our radical uniqueness, and all that means about myself, you, the world and God. It flows from and has led to the discovery of several deeply held convictions, which can be characterized as the meanings of uniqueness. These in turn are, I believe, the key to human identity. My convictions are briefly outlined below, and then explored in more depth throughout the rest of the work.

Only I can be me, and only you can be you

To reinforce the message we took from our encounter with Glyn, there is no one else in this universe that is quite like me, and there never will be again. This means that there are things in this world that only I can do. Exactly the same can be said of you. There are ways that only you can be, stories only you can tell, poems only I can write, songs only you can sing, conversations that only you and I can have together, interventions that only you can make. In short: I matter, and you matter. We are of infinite, cosmic significance. We are irreplaceable. Our identity lies in this, our uniqueness.

But my sense is that we live in a world where we are not appropriately in awe of the value of our own uniqueness, and we therefore lack a true sense of our own identity. And, just as importantly, we lack a true sense of the identity of others. We do not seem able to embrace, or to be enlarged and expanded through engagement with those who are different from us. And anybody and everybody is different from us. Rather, our tendency appears to be to fear the uniqueness of others and their consequent strangeness to us; to use other people as a means to a sense of our selves and our own importance. We do one of two things: we make them like us in order to contain the challenge of their difference, or we make them entirely 'other' and refuse to see any commonality. Both these approaches are, at root, forms of violence. We violate the other without thinking about it or realizing it. For this reason violence is often at the heart of our selves (in the form of self-hatred and destruction), our families (neglect and abuse) and our communities (civil strife and gang warfare).

You and I need one another

The flip side of our uniqueness is our profound limitation. Without others, each of us is but one small and isolated piece of a giant cosmic jigsaw. So there can be no separation between me and you. We need one another. We are interdependent.

The question is: how do I, as one unique and irreplaceable human being, step beyond myself and into an encounter with another unique and irreplaceable human being – you? What is the purpose of such an encounter, and what makes it good? Our globalized context furnishes us with ever-increasing opportunities for such communications, but there is little evidence that any significant difference is being made, for we still live in a world riven with injustice, inequality, conflict and misunderstanding. What are we called to in our encounter with the other? Is it understanding? Not if this means we reduce the other to someone who is just like us, for this violates that person's uniqueness. Is it simply a recognition of his or her mysteriousness and difference? Not if this leaves the other as an incomprehensible stranger, with apparently nothing to do with me.

A friend told me recently of her experience of sitting through an unsatisfactory theological conference session. The theme was 'otherness/alterity'. After an hour or so of abstract theological reasoning about the nature of 'the other', one of the participants – a Latin American woman from a liberation theology tradition – could bear it no longer. 'We don't call them "others",' she said. 'We call people "neighbours".'

Most of us will have experience of unhelpful encounters: manifesting indifference, misplaced sympathy, or inappropriate or patronizing concern-from-the-outside. Why do these apologies for interpersonal relationship feel so empty? Because they undermine our humanity. They fail to satisfy my desire to feel you as somehow a part of me; my sense that I should matter to you and vice versa. I want you to 'get it'; to understand; to 'get me'. I want you to see reality through my eyes, and to look back at me with recognition. I want you to let me in to who you are; to help me to understand you. When that happens, we feel intimate – connected. And we come alive.

The one-to-one encounter that is the most deeply personal, and personally challenging, is an exercise in the development of intimacy. But it is simultaneously a radical kind of political activity, for it engenders deep social change. Every time we forge an intimate connection with another person, a connection that honours the uniqueness of that person, we let go of something of our limitation and smallness. We change and expand and grow. We erode a stereotype, we leave behind prepackaged assumptions. Political oppression and prejudice rely on the tyranny of smallness, the promise of the preservation of stability and the value of what already fits in the palm of our hand, in contrast to the riches we might encounter by losing our grip. So intimacy, as explored in this book, is not simply about privatized one-to-one warm feelings for another that offer comfort and succour. Rather, to embrace intimate connections is, ultimately, about hard-edged social transformation. We might call this 'intimate neighbourliness', for as theologian Sebastian Moore puts it, 'intimacy cannot be regarded as a romantic notion. Intimacy should be regarded not as an insulation against a heartless world, but on the contrary as a wholesome contagion in a heartless world.'[1]

The most pervasive assumption about identity that circulates in the Western world is that the big identity question is 'Who am I?', as though we can answer that question without reference to anybody else. The next most popular and incorrect assumption is that 'who I am' is up to me – it is within my control. The spirit of our age considers the development of self-identity as a project to be managed. My task is to actualize myself, to make the right choices that will enable me to be the best that I can be. We are urged, explicitly and implicitly, to 'take control' of our lives, to 'be who we really are' (but also to reinvent ourselves at regular intervals. This is because we see ourselves as marketable commodities, and the customer is easily bored).

Of course there are certain important choices that we make for ourselves. And there are options always before us about how the person we have become, through an impossibly mysterious and complex interaction of people, events, history, physical and emotional make-up, personality type, nature/nurture, cultural influences, etc., can be in the world. But the notion that we are each discrete self-defining and self-determining beings, in charge of the future and of our own self-project, is a travesty of the mystery of what it means to be human.

We belong to God

> . . . *the mysterious energy that flows between persons, is what opens us to God. It is at once the opening of our desire to God and God's point of entry into us; our way of opening, God's way of entering.*
>
> Sebastian Moore[2]

It is my conviction that our uniqueness is intended. It is divine gift. We are meant to revel in it, to love ourselves and appreciate our glorious one-offness. To the extent that we embrace our uniqueness, God is delighted, and as we stretch out towards intimacy with others, God's passion is alight. But for most of us, these are the hardest, simplest spiritual lessons we will ever (and never completely) learn.

Interestingly, it is a feminist theorist with no explicitly spiritual intent who introduces God to us as 'G.O.D: the Generator Of Diversity'.[3] Donna Haraway is right, for the creative force at the heart of the universe seems to be one that cannot get enough of difference. Think how hard it is to produce two or more things that are the same. Not even the office photocopier or laser printer can manage exact and perfect replicas. There are too many variables (quality of paper, temperature and humidity of the room, angle of the autofeed, temperament of the machine). How much harder it is to conceive of two human beings that are exactly the same. Observe how identical twins – with their perfectly matching genetic make-up – blossom into difference from one another from the moment of their conception.

How we live our uniqueness is a deeply spiritual question, for it invokes notions of ultimate meaning, value and purpose. When I struggle with who I am, what I am for, and by whom I

am loved (all frequent occurrences), I find it helps to move outwards – to stretch beyond the 'I' to the 'we', and to stretch beyond
the 'we' to that which is vast and mysterious: sky, stars, the sea,
the crowds. This has two contradictory effects. First I feel small
and potentially insignificant. In the scheme of things, what do I
matter? Second, though, I feel an acute yet simple need to be
beheld by another – to see and be seen, at all of the various levels
involved in that process. Just an-other, human or divine, or the
divine in the human. It is then that I feel, in a positive sense, 'put
in my place' – and I become someone. There are those without
whom I could not be who I am, and there are those who could
not be who they are without me. This matters. In a way, it is all
that matters, and God is somehow at its heart. To inhabit again
even the most fleeting connection of this kind has a transformational effect. Such connections speak of the divine, and the
divine is within them. Whatever the role of institutional religion
and conventional faith, the spiritual question remains: what is
our place in the world? And what more significant purpose
could there be to life than to be all that I can be because I, and
only I, can be it?

God's desire is that we be all that we can be

Let's go back to Glyn. The chances are that many things will
prevent him, as he grows, from being all that he can be. Perhaps
his passion will be for poetry, but his parents will pressurize him
into a future where financial security is valued above his creativity. Maybe he will make friends who will reject him if he refuses
to do as they do – experimenting with recreational drugs or
underage sex. He may be bullied at school and lose his self-
confidence. Or he may be fantastically successful when he grows
up, as a businessman or a scientist or a writer, but fail to find
someone who loves him unconditionally, and whom he can love
in return. What does this matter? And whose 'problem' is this? If
what we have said about human interdependence is true, then

this matters to each and every one of us, for something vital is lost to us all.

So we are returned to an exploration of our wider social context. What is the politics of identity in the culture of global capitalism that dominates our time? What can we see of the sea that we swim in?

First, our identity is forged through comparison and competition. We believe in our relative value, not in our inherent value. We attempt to 'be someone' by comparing ourselves favourably with others. But our insecurity elicits the opposite effect, for we find ourselves surrounded by those who (in our perception) have achieved more in life, earn more money, have a happier family life, a more tasteful and tidy home, and a better-looking partner. We become depressed by competition because there is no happy place to stand on ground that is constantly shifting.

Second, we are required, above all, to be economically productive units. In a profound sense, therefore, we are pressed out of shape by forces that require human beings to be uniform and predictable in order to serve the economy. This is not just about money, but about the way that we think – even the way we think about human psychology and development. Externality, tangibility and measurability are valued more highly than internality. What matters are definable outcomes and predictable results whether in business, medicine, education – or even religion.

We invest in material achievements because they are easier to measure. It's harder and harder to make a case in the public square for investment in intangibles – so we find it hard to value, for instance, the uniqueness of someone with a learning disability; the wisdom of age; the role of illness and vulnerability in the forward movement of our communities. We restrict the lessons we are willing to learn, and we exclude from our purview those from whom we think we can learn nothing. Or, worse, those who highlight for us the precariousness of our own identities formed through such value-systems. So we ignore homeless people and refugees, because all that stands between us and such a fate is luck, and we cannot bear to recognize this. We form ourselves as 'one to whom such a thing could never happen' rather than the more realistic, 'one to whom this could happen at any time'.

As we swim in this cultural sea, we develop strategies to prevent us from drowning or losing ourselves. Investment in personal autonomy and disengagement from others are two obvious ways of refusing to be affected by the erosion of a sense of our inherent value. We isolate ourselves, cut ourselves off. Paradoxically, one popular way of doing this in our culture is through an exclusive investment in nuclear families. This can be done in a way that undermines our sense of responsibility to wider social networks. In this way we hope that at least those closest to us will recognize and reinforce our identity as loveable and valuable human beings. But to do this we have to distance ourselves from other individuals and families. We care passionately about our own health and that of our children; our own careers and our children's education – and think that this is the entirety of our responsibility towards others. Putting our children first is the limited vision that now passes for altruism in our society. We call it living morally and decently. 'Looking after one's own' may be a way of embracing a slightly bigger world than simply looking after oneself, but the more it takes hold as an alternative to a more corporate approach that recognizes the interdependence of everyone on the planet, the less and less likely we are to ever again have political visions of health, education and flourishing for all.

Why is this book written as it is?

This is not just a 'head' book. It is a heart and soul book too. For reasons that will become clear, I consider stories to be at the heart of human identity. Story and analysis are therefore interwoven throughout. Not in the sense of offering a story and then analysing it – but bringing story and analysis together as alternative ways of exploring the same terrain; as different ways of looking at the same questions and issues. Both the stories and analysis in turn integrate, I hope, thinking and feeling – reason and emotion. The personal and reflective passages in the book represent my attempt to articulate an emotional landscape and its significance – a way into the 'felt self'. I use this as a shorthand designation for the complex interweaving of feelings, thoughts and stories that make up one's internal life. My instinct has been to lead with the felt self, and psychologist Carl Rogers helps me to understand why this has been the case:

> I have almost invariably found that the very feeling which has seemed to me most private, most personal, and hence most incomprehensible by others, has turned out to be an expression for which there is a resonance in many other people. It has led me to believe that what is most personal and unique in each one of us is probably the very element which would, if it were shared or expressed, speak most deeply to others. This has helped me to understand artists and poets as people who have dared to express the unique in themselves.[4]

There are several books that I might have written on the theme of identity. But this particular book is the one which, I feel, embodies in the writing the ideas it is aiming to express. I have articulated above my passionate commitment to finding ways to rediscover the value of human uniqueness as the bedrock of our identities. It has therefore been imperative that, as far as possible, I have written this book in a way that honours the uniqueness of my own personal experience, and offers that personal experience as a locus for connection with you, the reader.

I invite you to reflect on your own patterns of thought and feeling as you encounter what is written here – particularly what is written of the felt self. When you read my personal reflection, what are you doing with it, and how does it feel? Are you delighted or repulsed; comforted or afraid? Are you thinking to yourself, 'that is so much like my experience, it's scary'? And if so, are you projecting things on to my experience because you are assuming I am like you? Or are you thinking, 'I have no idea what this woman is saying. I can't imagine what it must be like to be her'? And if you are thinking these things, are you demonstrating how hard it is to appreciate the unique experience of another, on its own terms? And if you are doing *that*, what does this mean for the whole human endeavour of negotiating variegated identities in a complex world; trying to understand one another and negotiate our differences?

Why write this book at all?

Most of the key challenges of our time have, at their root, questions of identity. Global warming: who do we think we are as human beings, and how is it that our self-understanding has led us into the paradoxical situation where we appear to be on the brink of destroying our only home? World poverty: what limits do we put on our sense of responsibility for and to others and what does this mean about how we see ourselves? The war against terror: who are the people we call 'terrorists' and what is driving them? Do we have any idea? Have we bothered to find out, or have we simply decided they are a different species of human being, and we must therefore obliterate them? British democracy – a liberal, tolerant and decent society that everyone in the world wants to be part of: then why do we imprison our children, abuse our senior citizens and appear to know the cost of everything but the value of nothing? What are our real values, accidentally exposed?

And, closer to home: when someone asks who I am, how do I answer? I am a white, able-bodied, forty-something married woman who works for the Church of England and lives in London. What does this description say about me, and what does it leave out? What is the function of the identity categories, and can I do without them? Which ones can change, and how? Are there some that are unchangeable, and essential to who I am? What categorizations do I use in my mind when I meet others, and how do I value and violate those I encounter by these un-examined patterns of thought?

Much in the contemporary world of politics and the media is dominated by questions of identity. Would the cult of celebrity thrive as it does if each and every one of us (the masses; the public; the non-famous; those who are famous for fifteen minutes, then are trashed) was secure in our sense of our selves and convinced of our own value? Would the various kinds of tribalism that cause social conflict and strife be as entrenched if our sense of ourselves was less rigid? Would books like *Men Are From Mars, Women Are From Venus*[5] be massive best-sellers if there was no truth in them, and insofar as they contain important truths about gender identity and difference, are these differences that should be honoured and respected, or overcome? The identity questions of our time are about race, culture, religion, ethnicity, class, gender, sexuality, illness, age, nationality, personality type, ability and disability, heritage, personal story and experience, and the complex interaction between all of these. And that was not an exhaustive or comprehensive list!

And the territory where these identity categories overlap is the landscape that lurks between the personal and the political, the individual and the corporate. In understanding identity, these two must be held together in our minds at all times – in complex and creative tension. My forays into this landscape have led me to identify several paradoxes of identity that will hover in the background of every exploration in this book:

- I want to be free and unfettered/I want to belong.
- I am unique/I am like every other person.
- I am singular/I am plural.
- I am separate/I am interconnected and interdependent.
- I am consistently the same person/I am constantly changing and in flux.
- I am real/I present façades.

- I am the self I feel myself to be/I am the self I present to the world.
- I have a history that I value/I do not wish to be restricted by that history.
- I am my achievements/my achievements are not wholly mine.

It is already clear, then, that grappling with questions of identity is not a self-absorbed struggle with an individualized 'I-dentity' and its various crises. Rather, it is an ongoing conversation about all that it means to be a human being alongside other human beings, trying to make sense of one another and of our planet.

2

Others

⇒ ● ⇐

*We are never alone, but always 'face-to-face' with other people
who call us to recognize our responsibilities to them. 'To be I'
. . . signifies not being able to escape responsibility because
I am bound uniquely to the other.*

Emmanuel Levinas (paraphrased)[1]

Exploring difference

Face to face with you, I understand you perfectly, and not at all

In the beginning you were just a name uttered by a mutual
acquaintance (mispronounced, I discover). You were a
phone number on a post-it note that might never have
been followed up. Our first meeting was oddly conceived –
a transgression of the rules of my diary. Funny. Momentous.
Ordinary. Coffee in your flat, with immediate mutual trust
and surprising common ground. Why do we not pay more
attention at times like this? Something in your eyes offered
me memories of the future, and something of who we would
become to one another reached backwards offering safety
and reassurance, while gently pulling my life from under me.
Proof enough that human relating cannot be contained in
linear time.

You invite me into your world and I step forward eager,
yet afraid. What if I trample on that which I do not under-

stand, fail to see the value in what you deem precious, pay insufficient respect to your textured meanings? You trust me, and you beckon with warmth and recognition of the deep difference as though you have been here before. I guess you have been here many times, just not with me.

Our commitment is born early, and remains fierce. What is our commitment? Much of it is unspoken, much unknown, even to ourselves. For me, it goes something like this: to struggle to inhabit your world and not to run away, to resist always the pull to assume that my logic is your logic (easy to say. Very hard to achieve), to remind myself constantly that my attempts to systematize what I know of you will not work. Your excess will always intervene.

Knowing you is like walking in the same garden, but not always in your company: coming across you suddenly, as I round a corner; looking at you over a light-reflecting pool; following you into the labyrinth or the maze; observing together a scene of beauty (new blossom) or of devastation (death and degradation – present or past). In the garden there are places I cannot go with you, ways I cannot follow. You smile when this happens, though this bespeaks resignation rather than happiness. Knowing I could not go there, or wouldn't, you invited me anyway. I feel disappointing but loved, regardless. I know, then, that we belong in different places, which makes 'us' even more precious and surprising. I long to belong where you belong, but I never will. I yearn for you to belong where I belong, but know this cannot be. This is not about geography, it's about identity, and history, and choices.

Who we are to one another is our overlapping hinterlands. When first we met this land was a mere sliver – like the new moon. Yet that sacred place where our identities overlap has slowly extended itself through a process that feels difficult, sometimes, like creating – a work of art. In receiving you, I trace contours of your otherness, like fingers on skin tracing contours of the physical body. This is a psychic tracing, but visceral too. Like tasting food, one mouthful may be an accurate predictor of the next, but often it is not.

Glimpses of near-perfect connection punctuate our relationship. Clear-eyed and direct, this communication. Wordless, usually, it proffers firm places to stand and recover, to process and pay attention to the changes that have been wrought in me, by you, in you, by me. Where hinterlands overlap we feel safe – as one – I know you, you know me. The place of non-overlap is a place of challenge. You can't have one without the other. I visit as a stranger, handing in my passport, feeling vulnerable, stretching beyond myself. Our common hinterland grows, yet the unshared land is vital to it, and remains.

Hours and hours, days and days, face to face, we give one another attention: take notice, listen, hold back. Hours and hours, days and days, we slowly raise the stakes in our risk-taking. And why, after all of that, is it still so hard to trust that this love-locked land will not disappear? All we need to make it so is to trust that it will be so. This feels like a religion – a faith – in itself.

Imagine meeting someone for the first time. What happens? You put out a hand (having done your best to sense the appropriateness of this move). She takes it in hers. You notice whether the hand is warm or cold, the handshake firm or hesitant. She looks into your eyes: is this a sign of confidence or presumptuousness? Is she appreciating this or taking it as her entitlement? What if she doesn't look you in the eye? Or looks quickly, then away. Is it suspicion you see in this, or dislike, or the opposite: attraction – desire, even? Or perhaps it is simply a cultural imperative, or lack of confidence. If it's the latter, is it right to try to put her at her ease? That will depend on the circumstances – on the power relationship between you. It's an interviewer's job to put the interviewee at her ease, not vice versa. Vice versa makes you too sure of yourself.

What has this person heard about you and what is she expecting? While you wonder this, you are simultaneously reappraising what you've heard about her. Does it square with the evidence? Your mental picture is shifting: the anticipatory image is giving way to what your senses and instinct are creating as the encounter progresses. That's funny: I expected you to be younger/older; I had assumed you would be black/white; your name made me think you would be a man, so it's a real shock to me that you are a woman. I am recovering from this while holding up my end of the conversation.

Some psychologists and philosophers have argued that there is a particular trap that we fall into when we have a new experience. That is, we try to classify and categorize new (unfamiliar) things by comparing them with old (familiar) ones – noting the differences and the similarities. We grasp the new by the old. This trap extends to encountering other people – we grasp the 'not-I' by the 'I'. This means that we avoid the challenge of the 'not-I' by making him or her like ourselves. As a result, we learn only what we already know. As psychologist and theologian Peter Schmid puts it,

> all such learning is like 'grabbing'. We take possession of what we already know . . . we take something in order to 'include' it. We 'come to terms' (terminus, finishing point). We set limits. We overcome the difference and make the other a part of our own. Harmony and cohesion become more important than diversity and variety.[2]

This insight presents a deep challenge in the realm of interpersonal encounter, for the alternative approach Schmid puts forward is this: 'In encountering the other we need to start our thinking with the other, not with the self. We need not to include but to distance, not to grasp but to let loose. The challenge is to let them disclose themselves.'[3]

How on earth do we do that?

The suggestion is that what's at work within us in encountering a new person (or encountering a familiar person in a new way) is a kind of checking out: in what ways is this person like us, and therefore comprehensible to us, and in what ways are we challenged by his or her differences from us? Perhaps a good place to start, then, is with some excavation of the concepts of 'commonality' and 'difference'. These are common-sense notions that need further exploration. For what constitutes commonality? How do we perceive difference? Does difference necessarily make someone less comprehensible to us?

Imagine a typical social interaction: two adult men starting to get to know one another by talking about their children. Much social discourse focuses on adults' identity as parents. I know this because I am not a parent. 'Do you have children?' is commonly perceived to be an easy question to open a new encounter. It is, after all, assumed to be 'safe'. It isn't at all, of course, but we'll come to that later. Here's how such a conversation might unfold:

Adam: 'Do you have children?'
Peter: 'Yes, I have four.'
Adam: 'FOUR? Wow. I find it hard enough coping with two. How do you do it? Emma and William are eight and six. They . . .'

This interaction looks like an attempt at connection by establishing a commonality. But it isn't really. It's an excuse for one man to tell another man about his children. Adam asks a question, yes, but then immediately incorporates the response into his own experience of life. He takes possession of the 'not-I' by including it in the 'I', thus preventing further disclosure by the 'not-I' – that is, Peter. The message from Adam is: 'Wow, you have four children. I feel a bit threatened by this because it looks as though you have achieved rather more than I have. Never mind, I will cope with this by refusing to get inside your experience of having four children. Instead, I shall tell you what it's like

18

to have two children. In fact, to be precise, I will tell you what it's like to have *my* two children.'

It could've gone like this:

Adam: 'Wow, four children. How old are they?'
Peter: 'Well, two are grown up, the other two are under five.'
Adam: 'How interesting. What are the challenges in parenting when there's such a big age gap?' etc.

This time, Adam might learn something that he didn't know already – something about how it feels to be somebody else. Peter Schmid is right that most of us – for a whole host of reasons – find it easier to come to terms with the other by making him or her like ourselves; by refusing to open ourselves to experiences that are not our own. I know this as a non-parent who experiences these common-sense, supposedly safe, 'getting to know you' conversations from a minority position (or what feels like a minority position). If I'm not careful, I find myself mentally switching off from someone else's tales of their offspring by offering mere reactive tolerance and no proactive curiosity. In doing this I assume that I know pretty much what the person will say, and that I have nothing new or interesting to learn by listening to his or her experience. I have, I believe, got the other person safely slotted into my worldview. I am tempted to close down conversations about other people's children in order to avoid what might be a challenging engagement with their difference. For their life experience may call into question decisions and choices I have made which in turn have formed a somewhat precarious self-identity that I feel the need to protect. The choice is between 'closing down' and 'opening up'. Closing down is safe – opening up is risky.

There is something further at stake here, though, for it seems that as soon as we start to scratch the surface of an everyday interaction like this, we immediately trip up on power and politics. I notice, for instance, that a black friend with whom I have discussed our apparent commonality in knowing how it feels to be part of a minority grouping (albeit different minority group-ings), and therefore at times hated simply for being who we are, happily joins the ranks of the powerful majority when it comes to discussions about being a parent. Insofar as this has an alien-ating effect upon me, this is not a deliberate strategy on his part and it certainly isn't intentional. It is simply my feeling in response to yet another conversation where certain things about relational lifestyle are taken to be normative – highlighting, sometimes in unsettling ways, my identity as someone who has not made normative choices. There will be other occasions, no doubt, when he will observe me at home with my normativities – for instance, my whiteness. Whether this elicits feelings of alienation on his part I cannot say. But this example underlines the fact that the whole point about normativity is that it is based on an assumption that there are certain things we all share (e.g. knowing what it's like to get married, to know who your parents are, how it is to have an extended family, how it feels to be a parent), whereas in fact there are few things we all share. The common-sense assumptions at the heart of conversations are everywhere and frequently causing feelings of alienation and despair. How can we learn not to make them?

So discussions about commonality and difference must take account of the wider social context in which they are set: who and what is valued and devalued, rewarded and punished, and why. In other words, our closing down or opening up is not simply to be understood in terms of individual courage or cowardice. They have a political dimension that is extremely important. How and in what ways we feel able to open up, and how and in what ways we find it necessary to close down will be the result of past experiences of empowerment and disempow-erment. And how we have responded to such experiences will in turn depend on our unique personal combination of emotional and psychological coping mechanisms.

Insofar as we do not share in the common-sense world of the powerful majority we may be considered (and may consider ourselves) to be part of 'a minority' and may join with other people with a similar experience in order to obviate the effects of feeling left out, devalued and misunderstood. It's helpful sometimes to be in a social context where the common-sense world of the majority does not hold sway (e.g. a gay club, if you are gay). Interestingly, however, what then unfolds are the many ways in which commonality in one part of life does not extend to commonality in other parts of life. This is at the root of the problems that emerged in what used to be called 'identity politics'. For instance, women who forged political movements based on the perceived shared experience of being women discovered that racial and sexuality differences (among others) were often problematic and too important to ignore, and 'gay and lesbian' groups discovered that gender differences between gay men and lesbian women made it difficult to come up with a common agenda for social change.

So commonality and difference are much more complex than first appears. The comparison between self and other that is taking place at various levels in both of us when I encounter you is about our sense of one another as individuals, yes. But the bigger picture within which this encounter is set is that of I-as-a-social-being meeting with you-as-a-social-being. Both of us are bringing complex social mores and expectations into the equation.

A key question is: why do we assume that having something in common with another person makes it easier to establish a relationship with that person? And why do we think that difference in itself is an obstacle to intimacy? Perhaps this too goes back to the tendency to try to grasp the not-I through the I. For if we tend to form our relationships in this way, then the smaller the difference between the I and the not-I, the easier that task can be assumed to be. Most of us find it easier to open up more with those with whom we feel safe. And often we feel safe with those whom we assume to be like us. Or, perhaps more accurately, we feel safe with those who are like others with whom we have, in the past, felt safe. So, for example, if our life experience has taught us that women are trustworthy emotional confidantes and men are not, we will tend to open up about our feelings with women, and close down with men.

But the very complexity and slipperiness of commonality and difference, as explored above, calls into question any notion that we can really know, in advance of embarking on a relationship, how each will play itself out. I can know certain externally observable things about another person (his or her skin colour, apparent gender, level of physical attractiveness to me, and so on), but the significance and meaning of these cannot be known until a relationship has depth. The only 'knowing' we can have at first is an abstract and rational, reasonable knowing. The visceral and emotional appreciation of the meaning of our differences comes later, when consideration of such things is mixed up with the negotiation of everything else, visible and invisible, that makes us who we are.

Beyond commonality

Face to face with you, you walk away

It was an impulse, that's all. Get up, cross the room, sit closer. Be closer to the person who feels, at this moment, too far away. The emotional content of our conversation assumes intimacy; the space between us signals distance. I feel the urge to overcome the dissonance. In all the many months we have known one another, we have experienced not a single moment of physical contact. Is that not odd? Meetings and departures have been curious stand-offs. I sense uneasiness and avoidance, and part of me wants to understand this – another part of me is scared. This moment is now long ago, but my memory recalls (recreates?) the detail. I know how I was sitting and what I was wearing. It was summer. Evening was passing into night.

I stayed where I was.

Something in me felt a depth-charge of significance in this decision, yet I let the moment pass without remark, pass into a future of 'what ifs'. What if I'd got up and sat next to you on the sofa? What if we had touched? Or, what if I had vocalized my desire and simply said, 'You feel too far away. May I sit by you?'

But I talked of other things instead – surface things, easier things – and pushed my feelings away to a 'safe' place, thinking they would be there to analyse later.

I remained where I was because I was afraid. Afraid of rejection, afraid of what might ensue. I was frightened of the power of the feelings I refused to feel. I was frightened that you would feel the same, frightened that you would not. My mind was so far ahead in its conjecture that I had lived several alternative lives in the space of making that one simple decision: to move, or to stay still.

Alternative lives spun from privatized assumptions are, I know now, dangerous illusions. Reality may be uncomfortable, but at least it has foundations – in words spoken and, at least partially, understood. Spiralling out of control comes from not speaking the truth. So why is it so hard to speak?

Chaos erupted anyway, eventually, instigated by you. You love me, you say. You cannot love me, I say, you love someone else. And so do I. I will not follow where you want to go. My resistance is as strong as my instinct for survival. I want to protect others – and myself, of course. My feelings are irrelevant to the outcome I desire (by which I mean, intend), so I cannot afford to know them. Yet, I do know them. For they echo to me from memories of a hundred occasions.

I could not and did not hear your expressions of love when they came, what they meant, how they felt, from within your register, for you. Instead, I colonized them. I forced the feelings into a new shape – of how I would feel if I were you. I recast your meanings according to my analysis of what this would mean for me if I were you. I forgot that I am not you, and so I was fatally lost. I did violence to you and to myself. I was the totalizing force that would bring everything into line; make everything OK. Suppressing love, refusing embrace, digging channels, making dams, hoping that the water would follow the course I determined. This was a fierce and brutal reordering of reality. It was all for very good moral reasons, you understand. For the best of moral reasons.

Suddenly denying someone three times seems like a minor contravention. Only three times?

And, in the end (not surprisingly), you walked away. Back to your life, leaving me to go back to mine, as though nothing had happened. The pain was like nothing I had ever known, and it faded so slowly – as with all loss unresolved. Many years ago, but still it can be chokingly real. As now.

Recall how it feels to hit it off with someone instantly, even when that person is apparently (e.g. visibly) different from you, or has little in common with you. Powerful connection (or the felt potential for it) can be evident right from the start, and may have nothing to do with identity categories, commonalities and differences. It has everything to do, in my experience, with intuition, passion and desire. Indeed, one can feel bewildered and confused at the strength and power of a sudden, unexpected, mutual attraction. The commitment comes first, with no particular rational basis, and the process of encounter follows. There is a desire to know and be known. Who is the other? Where has she come from, what is her story and how has she become who she is? And there is a desire to disclose in equal measure. To say, 'This is me! This is who I am. Here are the things that have shaped me and formed me. Understand them!'

Equally, there can be occasions when, for no apparent

rational reason, one resists being drawn into a relationship with someone. Again, this can be an instinctive feeling that someone cannot be trusted; that one shouldn't give too much away – that one is somehow at risk. Most relationships fall somewhere between these two poles. When I tell my story to a new acquaintance, therefore, unless I am bowled over by an immediate sense of safety and instant trust, or I am exceptionally courageous (or reckless?), I rarely tell it straightforwardly. I emphasize the bits I think the other person will relate to most closely. I may even omit bits that I assume he or she will find difficult or challenging, particularly if the person I am talking to is someone who, for whatever reason, has more power than me, or has some measure of power over me (and therefore, for my own good, needs to be won over). In other words, my story depends, to some extent, on who I am telling it to. At the same time, however, I also know from experience that the strongest bonds are forged when I do not save up truth for 'later', and where difference and transparency can be accommodated right from the start. We are back, therefore, in that powerful nexus where our unique individuality – with its complex mix of robustness and vulnerability based on past experience – meets the political and social reality of power, which is beyond our control. The relational task that faces us in our encounter with the other is one of negotiation. We negotiate the risks inherent in opening up, but also the risks of what might be lost to us (self and other) if we close down.

Let us return, then, to the question of how we 'start our thinking with the other, not with the self' (to revisit Schmid's words). Perhaps the key to this lies not in thinking at all, but in feeling. Certainly feelings and emotions have to be part of the equation if we are to grasp the other as the other, without making him or her first like us. For we have to enter the feeling world of the other and be able to make sense of it and in it. Not to the exclusion of thinking, but perhaps to the exclusion of our learned assumptions and habitual responses. If we are not to make others like ourselves, yet still to make a connection (it is, after all, easy enough simply to avoid meaningful contact altogether – to remain completely indifferent to another), we have to move out of our world and into theirs. We have to do this while still recognizing their world as theirs, and our world as ours – otherwise we are simply lost, and no longer an 'other' at all. But any meaningful interaction will call us both to be changed by the experience.

Entering into the feeling world of another involves, I would argue, learning to appreciate the dynamics of empowerment/disempowerment that have formed them. We have not simply to understand the other as an individual with a unique psychological and emotional character, but we also have to learn to appreciate how the social and political backdrop of his or her life has impacted upon that unique character, and how it continues to do so. This is hard, because it is a realm where it is particularly tempting to assume commonality where there is none. Say, for instance, I get very close to someone who has experienced childhood sexual abuse. When I meet another person who has had a similar experience of disempowerment, I may think that I know a lot about that person already, because I already know someone else with that experience, and can draw parallels. But I will soon discover that human uniqueness disqualifies all such easy shortcuts. While there may be similarities in the experiences of disempowerment, no two people will respond to that disempowerment in the same way. I have to encounter each person completely anew.

Entering into the feeling world of another is a complex, subtle and extremely demanding task. I would like to suggest that it involves three very important characteristics – or perhaps they are learned skills – that we will come back to repeatedly in our grappling with the notion of human identity. These are: courage, emotional imagination and humility.

Courage comes first because, without it, we could not reach out to another at all. Reaching out often involves asking a question of someone – either verbally, or in some other way. To ask questions makes one vulnerable. It is in asking that we take a risk. There is always an element of uncertainty. What if the other reacts badly to our approach? What if she considers our question intrusive, inappropriate or silly? Or what if it becomes clear that she has waited a lifetime for precisely *that* question? Can we adequately bear the depth and overwhelming emotionality of the response? That's why asking questions is so important to finding out who the other is, and is therefore crucial to gaining insights into who we are. It takes courage to ask a question of someone because we may – at any time – encounter a life-changing insight; a deeply challenging or moving articulation of reality. Furthermore, we may fear that a response is expected from us, and we may feel inadequate to the task. Such anxieties spring from an obsession in our culture with activity and 'problem solving'. We feel we are being called upon to *do* something, to come up with answers and solutions, though usually all that is necessary is to listen, to be with; to witness to the truth as the other sees it. The courage to be present alone will enable stories to be told in new ways; feelings and realities to be articulated differently. That is enough for change to happen. So why are we afraid?

As I reflect on my upbringing, I discover that little attention has been given to the skills of asking questions of other people. My education has prepared me to assess evidence, weigh up options, make choices for myself, and communicate those to others. That is, I am well able to tell people things. But when it comes to asking, I find I am fearful. I have to take a deep breath before I do it. Every time, even now, after years of attempted unlearning. My cultural heritage is a strange one of 'minding my own business', which ignores the obvious fact that most people love to talk about themselves, have a powerful need to communicate their own story, blossoming and growing through it.

If our social context prioritizes telling over asking, it also prioritizes thinking over feeling, and therefore downplays the significance of what I am calling emotional imagination. We assume that we get to know others through finding out how and what they think, what their opinions and beliefs are – usually through discussion, debate and argument. But it's perfectly possible to have a lively and wide-ranging discussion with somebody, to be very clear by the end of it about how that person's mind works, while having no sense of his or her real identity – no sense that one has encountered his or her personhood.

Really knowing somebody comes from a sense of a growing familiarity with her emotional landscape. What is it that brings tears of sadness to her eyes? When is she delighted, and what makes her respond with joy, anger, frustration or impatience? Knowledge of the other begins to emerge, for instance, when my observation that she seems to be feeling sad accords with her confirmation that she is actually feeling sad. Human beings have a commonality (on the whole) in the tendency to feel sad at times, but there is a vast difference between what makes one person sad and what makes another sad; the ways in which this happens, and the ways in which each demonstrates that it is happening. The role of what I have termed emotional imagination lies in helping me to understand the dynamics of feeling in another. These dynamics may be completely unlike my own. For the interplay of empowerment, disempowerment and personal make-up are inherent in this. There is a certain assumed commonality in knowing what an emotion feels like (how else could human beings connect at all?), though its subtleties still need to be expressed (not necessarily in words), but the other person's uniqueness expresses itself in how and why and when that person feels an emotion, and how and why and when this emotion changes and transforms into something else. Imagination is the key to sensing these things in others. Imagination is the tool available to human beings that enables us to appreciate, to some degree, another's reality while also knowing that we will never actually experience that reality for ourselves in exactly the same way. Imagination is not about 'making things up', but about creatively entering into the reality of another, and recognizing that this reality lies beyond oneself and one's own self-understanding.

Emotional imagination is at the heart of human solidarity. It enables me to be open to your experiences and your story in such a way that I can learn from them without having to live through them myself. It enables me to learn appropriately – that is, at a level of my being which is not superficial or merely intellectual, but visceral. Emotional imagination in action is playful (even when encountering things that are deadly serious), generous and non-defensive. Play is that which takes us out of ourselves – and emotional imagination does just that. The crucial distinction to be made, however, is between one's own story and that of the other. However comfortable one begins to feel with the reality of another, this distinction remains, for without it, we fail to honour the other's uniqueness and instead make him or her an extension of ourselves. We offend against humility.

Humility derives from an acute awareness of the limits of our experience and of our understanding. It is not self-deprecation or an under-valuing of self, but quite the opposite. I can know another only within the limits (or at the limits of) what my current self allows. Though our potential for knowing another is, I would argue, usually much more capacious than our intellect alone would entertain. Yet I can know another only within the limits or at the limits of what the other person wants to give of him- or herself. Our knowledge of the other is always partial, with potential for growth and change. There is always so much more to discover and to learn, and there are surprises, and surprising new ways in which we can learn if we allow ourselves.

Who is my other?

Face to face with you, I am none the wiser

Always you deflect and defend. There are many versions of you. I meet you all the time. I feel profoundly alone in your presence.

Many of you are fierce. Your energy and vigour burn.

Survival depends on giving nothing away, showing no 'weakness'. There is no way in, no way through. You prickle and crackle with determination to face down efforts at penetration. Confrontation provokes tirade, circumlocution begets monosyllables of certainty. 'Were you happy about that?', 'Yes.' 'You must have been disappointed?', 'No, not at all.'

Open questions fail too. Your response implies that you think the enquiry nonsense, the answer self-evident; the question, therefore, surplus to requirements. And by implication, the questioner too (though that is, of course, the voice of my own insecurity). For what you hear is a request for information, when what is offered is an invitation to connect.

Some of you are friendly, offering a soft and constantly bubbling stream of apparent communication. But I soon discover this to be defence through distraction, a cunning emotional sleight of hand. You are a magician, master of the emotional illusion of closeness and easy intimacy. Catching my attention with engaging banter, you are elsewhere simultaneously whipping yourself out of sight. Swept away to safety in an instant. I see a lot of you at first, then nothing more. You are an easy win, but a pyrrhic victory.

Others among you are clever. Your repartee is polished from years of practice. Your hiding has a rhythmic cadence, an intellectual acuity and a vast knowledge base on which to draw. You never miss a beat or an opportunity. Your allusions come thick and fast. You test me through them. Am I worthy of connection with you? Do I pass? Have I made it? Will I ever know? With some of you, I pass. The reward is a bar set higher. With some I fail. I see a flicker in your eyes then as victory meets disappointment. The end is a dismissal.

Some of you I retreat from immediately, others I face up to on equal terms – joke meets joke; intellectual point-scoring meets showing-off. Sometimes I fear that I am one of you after all, and that my defensiveness is the origin, not the result. Sometimes I go away stimulated, but also empty, deprived. I feel frustrated. And yet I wonder: why am I always reactive in your presence? How come I cannot shake you or affect you? *I want to move you. Why?*

We have so far explored something of what happens when we encounter another. We have appreciated the temptation to close down and limit our engagement with another by, in effect, making that person like ourselves. We have discovered that each of us is a social being as well as a unique individual. That means that we are each located within a complex web of power structures, though the full significance of this is not always visible to us. These power structures bite, having profound effects upon our sense of ourselves, who we are and what we can achieve; and upon our sense of others, who they are, and what they are capable of. We have discerned three key characteristics that may offer us a way forward in creative encounter with others: courage, emotional imagination and humility.

A fruitful next step is to explore what happens in the absence of these three characteristics. For when any or all of these three things fails we are, I think, out of the realm of 'encountering' and into the realm of 'othering'.

Ask yourself this question: who is my other?

Who or what springs to mind? Is it someone you distrust, are intimidated by, cannot relate to? Is it someone or a group that is strange to you, that you do not immediately understand? Or is the 'otherness' about how the logic of his life fits together, that is not yours? Is it his motivations and values – about what makes him do what he does? Or is it more basic than that? Is it his outward appearance and all that you associate with it – the ghosts of your past exerting an influence in the present?

We are most familiar with the concept of 'othering' in a political context. It describes the dynamic by which groups with greater power define society's common-sense perceptions of reality ('We' are like this. 'We' are normal), using that power to define the characteristics of another grouping with less power, and therefore less ability to challenge those consequent perceptions ('They' are different. 'They' are not normal). We are also familiar with the 'othering' that lies behind scapegoating. In this case differences that are specific to a vulnerable minority (whether they be racial, cultural or simply experiential) are exploited and exaggerated to such an extent that the majority begins to objectify the minority and to believe that it has no commonality at all with them. At this point all humility about the limits of one's ability to understand another has been abandoned, so the blame for society's ills can be loaded on to the minority without fear of resistance by the majority. And courage is now rare among members of the majority, for they are not interested in asking whether their high-handed definition of the other is in any way accurate.

To the extent that we inhabit positions of relative power and privilege, we do not need to understand 'the other' for our survival. We do not need to employ emotional imagination to get on in life, because life goes pretty much our way anyway (though this may be invisible to us). And because emotional imagination is hard work, and most of us are pretty lazy (especially when it comes to the choice between simply accepting our privileges, and making the ongoing effort to be alert to them and challenge them), we don't bother unless we have to. Take, for instance, the example of a white person in a workplace where white people are in the majority. She may choose to try to understand institutional racism: how it operates in her work context, and what she might do to challenge it. But she is likely to face no obvious disadvantages if she doesn't bother to do that. If, however, she one day finds herself for the first time working closely with a black colleague, it is likely that she will discover the need to unlearn the covert racist messages she has received from society, which will be challenged by the actual encounter with a real-life multifaceted unique individual.

Those who belong to groupings that have less power, by contrast, have no option but to make the effort to understand 'the other', for society is run by and for the other, and in order to survive in that society they have to develop a keen and instinctive understanding of how the other works. That's why (to generalize wildly) women know more about men than vice versa; black people know more about white people, and gay people know more about straight people. Othering has lopsided results in terms of the extent of our understanding of others. Those with experiences of disempowerment and vulnerability tend to have better developed skills in emotional imagination – though it would be foolish to say that such experiences necessarily lead to that result.

But othering can also be an interpersonal dynamic between those who inhabit similar positions within society's complex hierarchies of structural power, and who might otherwise be assumed to demonstrate a kind of 'solidarity of the same'. Sometimes those who appear to be most like us to the casual observer (and most of us are, most of the time, little more than casual observers) may also be our 'others'. We may simply not warm to or like those that may be perceived to be most like us. And there may be complex political dynamics at the root of this. In a male-dominated workplace, for instance, a sole woman might be expected to feel a natural affinity for a fellow woman when she takes up a new post. But the situation could equally work the other way. For what if the sole woman has become accustomed to the mixed blessing of that position? There may be disadvantages to it, but there may be advantages too. Sometimes she may feel lonely, misunderstood, marginalized. But she might also, sometimes, feel that she has novelty value: she gets more attention, and secretly she welcomes this. A second woman will deprive her of her status as 'the only one'. So there will be significant psychological barriers to her instantly welcoming her new female colleague. Apart from which she may have nothing in common with this person beyond their shared gender (which, after all, she also shares in her day-to-day life with 51 per cent of the world's population).

There are many complex dynamics – both personal and structural – at work in othering. This helps us to see that there are many reasons why we might resist entering imaginatively into the feeling world of another in order to encounter them; many reasons to abandon all humility and assume that we can know and explain another person and therefore decide to speak for them or over them. And there are many ways in which our courage can fail in opening ourselves to the possibility of being changed. There is always something to lose.

We may, for instance, engage in othering because of a sense of insecurity about who we are. In a materialist, performance- and success-focused culture there are many reasons for most of us to feel insecure and unworthy much of the time. And there are many reasons why the root of these feelings will be hidden from us and inaccessible to our understanding. Call it status anxiety, existential angst, adolescent turmoil, mid-life crisis, depression in old age, but the contextual reality for most of us is a sense of uneasiness with who we are, with no clear sense of why.

We are encouraged to equate our identity with our achievements, but our achievements are, at best, precarious, transient and relative. Insofar as we come to believe in them, we need then to reinforce that belief by assuming that the achievements are wholly ours: that we have struggled against the odds and that our rewards are justified. We do not believe in our inherent value, only in our relative value. Our relative value must be bolstered against encroachments from 'below' and we must insulate ourselves against the failure we feel when we observe those who are 'above' us – who have apparently achieved more. Both these processes are othering processes. We make ourselves unlike those in both categories – the better off and the worse off. It takes courage to resist these tendencies to distance ourselves from others.

It is clear that at the heart of tendencies to disconnect from others is an acute sense of the precariousness of our own identity, and that both personal and political forces are at work in

Others

this. An important question, then, is: what might constitute a
sure foundation for a sense of self that will enable us better to
connect with others?

I am what I desire

Face to face with you, I see a new way of being

This place where we lunch is the epitome of urban chic.
Two courses for a fixed price signals the deliberate
democratization of gastronomy. My dessert, chocolate torte,
arrives balanced on its point. An impossible, gravity-defying
triangle. At that moment, as though prompted by the
paradox of my pudding, you make your announcement –
with gusto and a candid, spoon-waving flourish:
'I want to be married and monogamous, and I desire to
sleep around.'
I laugh. Genuine delight seeps through me as the
implications of your announcement dawn, and an
excitement wells from my soul outwards. But the
implications have nothing to do with sexual ethics. No, this is
about the nature of wanting.
Is it . . . could it just be possible . . . to feel such obviously
contradictory emotions at the same time? If not, how could
such feelings be expressed with such apparent transparency?
Is it . . . could it be possible to accommodate (and with relish
– as I am relishing my dessert) desires that apparently pull in
diametrically opposed directions: feelings in mutual
contradiction? I see clearly in you, at that moment, that not
only is this possible, it can also be spoken. This is a sudden
and powerful liberation. I see this acknowledgement of
feeling as simply that. Precisely that. Only that. This is not
about what you will do, or how you will behave, it is simply
how you feel. It is simply, happily, true.
Later, I tell you how much I have learned from the way you

expressed yourself, and what you expressed. You are surprised. You say you did not know that I had learned from you, but that you are glad. You also say that you have learned that expressing feelings is important because through expression, they are changed.

It is often said, 'You are what you do.' It is much truer to say, 'You are what you feel.' It is in feeling happy, or angry, or sad, or hopeful, in response to an event, that I touch base with myself. My identity lights up in one of these feelings.

Sebastian Moore[4]

For a while I did a job that involved reading speeches by politicians – either before or after the event. These were always headed 'Check Against Delivery'. This intriguing phrase meant nothing to me, so I investigated its meaning. Apparently it's a warning to those (e.g. journalists) who might want to quote said minister or spokesperson: 'This is what I plan to say. Check it against what I actually say on the day' – i.e. against what is actually delivered.

I realize that much of my life has a 'check against delivery' dynamic to it. There's the 'me' or the 'self' that I plan in advance – that I set myself up to be, according to a huge range of influences (a bewildering and complex concoction: societal expectation and parental influence, which form my own aspirations, in turn shaped by my achievements and failures, revised all the time into modified hopes and ambitions). All of this adds up to a 'script' I feel I need to follow, or that I simply get used to following. The script declares: 'I am the kind of person who . . .', or 'I am not the kind of person who would ever . . . .' But lurking in the background all the time is the person who surprises me; the one who subverts that script. Which is the 'real' me? It is this question of authenticity that is at the heart of much of our insecurity about identity. Am I being 'real'? How do I know? Does it matter?

There are two similar but distinctive dynamics at work here.

First, we are all – to varying degrees – plural selves. Our range of selves and identities is related to the range of roles we play. The professional self, for instance, is different from the self a lover sees – which is different again from the self a parent or a child sees. Our sense of our own identity is, on the whole, well able to cope with this plurality as a necessary part of life. Having said that, there will be a way of inhabiting my 'professional' self that is authentic and true to me, and ways that are not. Ditto with my other selves and other roles. My uniqueness means that I can be this kind of mother and not that kind; this kind of lover and not that kind.

Related to this plurality, because we are social beings, we also have a range of 'presentational' selves. Anyone who behaves in exactly the same way regardless of who she is with, and whatever the situation, is rightly regarded as, at best, gauche, and at worst insensitive or dysfunctional. We each bring a repertoire of behaviour to the range of relationships we engage in. Only we (and those who know us best) can discern when we are being ourselves and when we are straying beyond the boundaries of what is authentic behaviour for us. In other words, our authenticity is self-defining.

So if plurality and living with a range of presentational selves are not themselves the problem, what is it that leads us to a sense of identity crisis? What are the causes of our anxiety or doubt about who we are? What leads us to lose a sense of ourselves ('I don't seem to know who I am any more. I feel lost'), and what is behind our worry about whether we are being authentic ('I really don't know whether that's ME')?

There may be several dynamics at work here. For instance, we may feel too narrowly restricted: perhaps the plurality of our roles is not broad enough, or the repertoire of how we present ourselves to others doesn't satisfy us. This may be because one strand of our plural identity is dominating all the others. For example, women who become mothers often comment that this aspect of their identity 'completely takes over' who they are – at least temporarily – and there is a massive internal readjustment that has to be made in the wake of this. Or if our job is overly demanding we may feel that our selfhood calcifies, with our professional persona as our single defining feature. In this case our sense of plurality is lost, or cannot be expressed to the extent that we would like. Or perhaps we are lonely and feel that we don't mix enough with others. Given that different aspects of who we are become evident according to who we are relating to, isolation might lead to a felt loss in the richness of our repertoire of personas.

Our sense of ourselves can be challenged when the categories that apply to us constrict us, or are applied too rigidly. We may feel we have 'grown out of' them but don't know how to communicate this to others. Or what if my presentational self is at odds with the person I experience myself to be? For instance, I may appear to be conventionally heterosexual but my desires may not accord with that label. How can I live this internal reality? How can my outside (how I may appear to others) come into line with my inside (the multi-faceted and ever-changing complexity of how I appear to myself)?

Or perhaps I simply feel unable to define myself, or lack the power to do so. I am, instead, the object of others' definitions of me. Society has labelled me, and I feel unable to escape a rigid categorization that I did not choose (e.g. I am mentally ill, homeless, a housewife, a refugee, a victim – of violence, disease, redundancy – you name it). If this is the case, my need is to feel self-defining again.

All of these examples raise for us the question: how can I be truly myself, and how do I know who is the real me?

Theologian Sebastian Moore makes a useful and fruitful distinction between the 'imaged self' and the 'felt self'. He refers to the former as the 'narcissistic self'. As he explains, 'The narcissist . . . is one who is out of touch with his/her true self, with the self that shows itself from moment to moment in feeling. He is fixed on a self of his own imaging.'[5]

The important difference between these two selves is that the narcissistic, imaged self is essentially privatized. He suggests that we each have a picture of ourselves hung in our private picture gallery, but this image is unavailable to everybody else. The 'felt self', by contrast, is potentially available and transparent to others. He says, 'the imaged self is always aloof from the scene, fearful of not receiving its due measure of adoration'.[6] In summary, he suggests that 'narcissism is not "having a grand image of myself as opposed to a modest image". It is "seeing myself in an image as opposed to feeling myself".'[7]

He suggests that narcissism (as he understands it) is difficult to escape in our current social context, for it is

> heavily endorsed by our society with its heavy emphasis on imaging ourselves. The vast, technologically empowered world of advertising stresses day and night the importance of being with the 'right' people, in the 'right' clothes, in the 'right' car, in the 'right' job, etc. I must be forever improving my image, learning more and more to see myself *in* the image of the good life.[8]

He suggests, however, that

> Once we begin to understand what it is in us that lets all this phony stuff in, we begin to see that we can overcome it. These voices of the culture, powerful though they are, are addressing a person who does not exist, namely a person who is known in the first place through a self-formed image . . . They are addressed to my non-existence, to my non-person.[9]

Moore's thinking brings us to a key paradox at the heart of human identity. For the primary characteristic of feelings is their mutability. They change all the time. So if the felt self is to be the foundation of our authenticity, then the conclusion must be that our real identities must be constantly shifting. In other words, though we are (on the whole) pretty much recognizable as the same person over time, we are also constantly changing. Just as you can recognize the same part of a river, or revisit a favourite stretch of ocean, yet the river and the ocean are constantly changing, so it is with human beings.

This means that the other with whom we interact is also a snapshot – unique to this time and to this place. Each opportunity for encounter is for now, and only for now. It is unrepeatable. What is more, if we are our felt selves, there can be no such thing as an encounter that does not change us. Each of us comes away changed from every encounter, because encounters make us feel. Sometimes (if the impact is particularly momentous) we notice it. Most often we do not. And sometimes the memory of an encounter can work its magic after the event, to reinforce its impact. We mull over what we said, what was said to us, how it felt then, how it feels now, what difference it made, what difference it might make in the future.

Perhaps this explains why we desire connection, but we fear desire; why we long to achieve a sense of our own individuality, but also long to be lost again in another. We are made for desire because we are made to be plural, dynamic, in flux, growing. We are not stable entities that come into contact or collision with other stable entities. We are processes that interact with other processes. This is the commonality that human beings share. We are not billiard balls glancing off one another, but rivers flowing in and out of one another. To quote Sebastian Moore again:

> human beings, beings in desire, in-exist one another, or they remain less than human, unfulfilled in essence. This is the universal fact about human beings. This it is which comes into play when two persons become intimate. When persons become intimate, they become what persons are . . . When two people become intimate, they join the human race.[10]

Perhaps, then, the learned skills we identified earlier in this chapter as being necessary to an appreciation of the feeling world of another can also be usefully understood as the skills of intimacy. Courage, emotional imagination and humility enable us to open up to another in ways that enable both of us to become more of what we can be. The skills of intimacy are crucial to the creative building of human identity because they are the skills of human connection, and connection gives us access to the 'we'. The more we access the 'we', the more fully human we become.

3

Power

We are our stories

I am visiting a family member whom I haven't seen for more
than a decade. He has a terminal illness. We don't know
today that his death is a mere three weeks away and that this
is the last time we will meet. Our question now is: how do
we catch up? How do we tell one another who we have
become in the time we have been out of touch? The ways in
which we have stayed the same are, perhaps, obvious. To him
it is how I look that is unchanged. He can't believe it – I say
it's not true. There is an externally defined ritual quality to
this exchange. The truth that hovers in its wake remains
unsaid – that the change in his appearance is drastic,
shocking, undeniable. It is the most tangible change; the one
I have been warned about, the one I most anticipated. Yet
within minutes it becomes the change that matters least.
More important is how unchanged and familiar is his
personality. He is the same person. He looks out at me with
the same eyes, through the same barbed-wire emotional
defences. But now I detect the presence of gaps; that a breach
of the boundary would not be unwelcome in his newfound
wilderness.

Beyond appearances, and behind the visible, all is story. He
tells me about his new family – who they are and what they
do. He tells me the story of his diagnosis and treatment: how
he discovered his illness, what it has meant for his life and

his plans. He tells me about the treatment that followed; the brutal practicalities of his transformation into a 'patient', and of what the doctors have said. And while the outcome of the treatment is at the moment unclear, I can see that he has hope . . . for more life.

There are stories of the hospice and his day visits – imbued with a sharp, well-rehearsed cynicism and humour. He tells me of the new hospice worker who has invited him to join her creative writing course. 'Creative writing?' he croaks, with incredulity. 'In a HOSPICE?! What the bloody hell do they think we've got to write about in here?' And the man who is full of stories declares unequivocally that he has no stories.

Finally, there are the photographs. Dozens laid before me on the coffee table, like sacred offerings on an altar, invoking the re-establishment of a connection; the re-forging of a familial bond. The effort and intention alone make clear that there is no need for this. The bond has never gone away. Yet this is an important gift – snapshots of memory of this latest (and, as it would turn out, last) phase of a life that I have not been part of. Here are people I do not know, places I have no idea he has visited – signs of a deep happiness that I did not know had visited him. Somewhere in this gift I sense mutual redemption – a way of both of us saying, 'I'm sorry,' and 'I know.'

Typically, when people first become friends they are eager . . . to tell one another about who they are, where they come from, what they have experienced. The experiences they exchange are not random, or complete. They tell those stories that explain or convey the person they are – 'I am what I have lived.' As people continue a friendship they are likely to spend some of their time retelling shared experiences. This is most common among friends who don't get to spend a lot of time together. Going over and over the same stories is a way of re-establishing connection, by re-establishing the past. For very

good friends who have done this a lot, the past becomes coded
with short phrases that stand for long stories.

Susan Engel[1]

When I was ten years old I was desperate to have pierced ears
and to wear earrings. My parents forbade it. Not simply on the
grounds that I was too young, but on the grounds that it went
beyond the bounds of acceptability for 'someone like me'. This
was something I sensed and felt, rather than something that was
ever explicitly stated, but it left me confused. Who was I in the
midst of this debate? Why was it not acceptable for me to have
piercings in my ears, when it was apparently uncontroversial for
other girls to have them? Did I have a different calling? Was I different, and if so, why? I didn't feel different from my friends, so
why must I look different? There seemed to me to be no defen-
sible rationale behind my parents' decision. Though I wouldn't
have put these words to it then, their perspective felt like some
sort of primitive purity law, irrelevant to my sense of identity as
a child of the 1970s. My sense of anomie was heightened further
by the fact that my best friend at school, Jane, was positively
encouraged to have her ears pierced. For Jane's parents, this particular kind of body piercing was not unnatural or a transgression into impurity. Far from it – it was a perfectly respectable rite
of passage for a girl as she embraced her femininity and adorned
herself with jewellery. The irony was, predictably, that Jane wasn't
particularly keen to undergo this rite. She thought it would hurt.
So while I was pestering my mother for permission to undergo
pain voluntarily, Jane had to be bribed by hers with the prospect
of being bought 'some nice little earrings'. I remember these
precise words very well. Or I think I do.

To add insult to injury, I was invited to accompany Jane and
her sister to the shop where their ear piercing took place. There
was a ceremonial quality to the whole thing. I witnessed the
deed, their pain, their tears, and wondered whether I did, after
all, wish it for myself.

In early adulthood, as a student, I recounted this tale to my new best friend at university (let's call her Rachel). She had also faced a parental banning of pierced ears, and we were exploring the significance of this commonality. In the telling, however, my story functioned in both of the ways outlined by Susan Engel in the opening quote. First, I told it in order to give Rachel an insight into my identity. It was indeed an example of 'I am what I have lived', and as we explored the story, the many-layered nature of its significance began to dawn on me. Indeed, things were revealed to me in telling the story *to Rachel* that would not have been revealed in telling it to someone else. For Rachel had German parents and had spent much of her childhood in the USA. She therefore brought an acute and astute outsider's analysis to my English childhood situation. As she laughed at my rendition of Jane's parents' promise of 'nice little earrings' (told, I have to say, in a somewhat snobbish mimicry of their estuary English), I began to see (with some shame) that there was something complex at work here related to the vagaries of the English class system. I began to see how differently structured could be the lives of two British white girls of roughly similar financial means, born in the same month, living in the same town, participating in the same state education system. And I began to see that power is complex and its workings are more mosaic than linear. Shards of it intrude, not always in a predictable or consistent way.

Suddenly the debate about earrings took its place alongside various other differences between Jane and me that had not been consciously real to me hitherto: the fact that Jane's dad was a builder and mine was a clergyman; her mum was a hairdresser and mine was a teacher; they lived on a housing estate in a modern bungalow with thick carpets and central heating (the object of my envy) and I lived in a big old detached house with threadbare carpets and gas fires; Jane had no books in her house and we had lots; Jane's mum bought cakes and my mum made them; they had a posh television and hifi and we had Scrabble and Monopoly; they had a half-moon squashy leather sofa and we had the kind of chairs you found in residential care homes for older people; we went on holiday to Scotland and Wales and climbed mountains, they went on holiday to Butlins (with no road atlas and got lost, whereas we always followed a meticulously pre-planned and well-researched route); Jane wore all the latest fashions and my clothes were run up on my mum's sewing machine, and my shoes always had to be 'sensible'; and finally, when we were 11 years old Jane went to the local secondary modern school and I went to the grammar, and that's how our friendship ended.

The second function of the story of the earrings, though, was the very fact that it became, for Rachel and me, and probably for ever, 'the earring story'. It was told and retold as part of the collective memory of our friendship, and in such a way that it became shorter and shorter, and the coded phrase that now stands for so much more is 'nice little earrings'. There are many such stories, and a multitude of shorthands, at the heart of our friendship. And my life, like most people's lives, is a multitude of friendships, acquaintances and connections, with stories at the heart of them all.

In her book on memory, *Context is Everything*, Susan Engel says that 'Personal identity is built, shaped, unmade and remade through the telling of stories.'[2] We have our own personal stories (like the ones told above), and our personal responses to the bigger, public stories that are taking shape all around us, all of the time (which wars do you remember? In what ways were you part of them? Where were you when Kennedy was shot? What were you doing on September 11, 2001? Do you remember the drought of 1976? And even as I write these questions, I realize how culturally specific and timebound they are). It seems that memory both creates, and is created by, story. Engel explains:

There are several layers of the phenomenon we refer to as memory, and recent years have brought great advances in what we know about almost all of these layers . . . Several parts of the brain have been identified for their role in one kind of memory or another. In addition, we now know that people build up neural pathways for memories, and that the more often that particular memory is invoked, the more solid and strong that neural pathway becomes. We also know that the neural mechanisms that lead to memory are very similar to the neural mechanisms used for imagining things. This has suggested to some that there is a physio-logical basis for the complex interweaving of fact and fiction in people's personal recall.[3]

Engel goes on to say:

Research has now shown that . . . retrieval is almost always more a process of construction than one of simple retrieval. One creates the memory at the moment one needs it, rather then merely pulling out an intact item, image, or story. This suggests that each time we say or imagine something from our past we are putting it together from bits and pieces that may have, until now, been stored separately. Herein lies the reason why it is the rule rather than the exception for people to change, add, and delete things from a remembered event.[4]

It seems, then, that memory is less about an objective recall of facts, more a creative, personal and imaginative process of iden-tity construction.

Perhaps this explains the pleasure that is often at the heart of personal story-telling, and the attraction of listening to the stories of others. Researching one's family tree is increasingly popular because it gives one access to a personal story that goes beyond oneself and spans previous generations: making other times and places a part of oneself. It is particularly interesting to note the heightened popularity of this at a time of increased individualism within our culture. As we have fewer meaningful links with others here and now, we delve into the past for that sense of connection. Another phenomenon is the role of memory boxes and personal reminiscence in the care of older people. As memories fail and old friends die, a box of items symbolic of the different facets of one's life can be a way into recreating memories and stories – giving a renewed sense of meaning.

Through these activities we are 'put in our place'. We find a sense of belonging and purpose. Story-telling and reminiscence are at the heart of human identity for both young and old. Poring over a photograph album or a box of old 'stuff' from the attic can be a way of connecting with who we are at a very deep level. Often this is pleasurable. Perhaps more often it is a bittersweet experience combining pleasure, bemusement, anger, regret, and the reliving of the whole gamut and complexity of emotion that accompanied the events we are remembering. Whatever the mix of emotions, in remembering (retelling our stories to ourselves) we certainly feel alive.

Indeed, according to Engel, what matters most about people's past is what they thought and felt. These feelings and thoughts centre around events (a move to a new town, the birth of a baby brother, experiencing a painful accident, getting married, living through a tornado), but at the crux of a memory are the feelings and thoughts that surround the action.[5] This fits well with our conclusion in Chapter 2 that the 'felt self', for all its constant change and flux, is the foundation of our authenticity – that (as theologian Sebastian Moore has it) we are what we feel, and what we remember that we felt, not what we do.

Interestingly, Engel also says this:

> We all tend to put ourselves at the center of the past. Why else create one? Why else remember? Even when we recall events that had ramifications for others, events in which we played a small part, we tend to magnify our own role and shift things so that they more directly relate to us . . . The self tends to appear more central, more important, and have

more of an impact than what 'really happened.' If five people were involved in an event, each will tell of that event so that he or she, the teller, appears as the central character.[6]

It is tempting to interpret this in a negative way – as a symptom of our incurable human egotism. But what if we interpret it as a wholesome tendency; as part of the innate and powerful human desire to matter and to be significant to others beyond ourselves? In her exploration of how memory is constructed after important public events, Engel describes how telling and trading stories about what happened becomes in itself a sequel to what happened. The comparing and melding of stories helps a community to come to a shared sense of an event. It also allows people to *participate*, if only through the activity of recollection, in the drama itself.[7] This insight could have significant and positive implications in a society characterized by loneliness and a sense of meaninglessness and purposelessness. Engel's insights point up for us the fact that each of us needs to feel that we matter – that we are participants in the life and the changes that surround us, not simply bit-parts or voyeurs. A fast-moving media culture exacerbates our sense that we cannot affect the stories that are formed by others for us to consume. A renewed culture of intentional story-telling might be the key to the reinvigoration of options beyond isolation and voyeurism.

Stories are not 'innocent'

The focus of this chapter is power. I have taken time to explore in some depth the relationship between story and human identity, for it is the fact that we 'are our stories' that highlights our uniqueness. Our stories are, therefore, the origin of our empowerment. But it is also in exploring our stories that we see most clearly the impact upon us of power structures that are beyond us, and external to us. Power issues saturate the memory-imbued world of our stories. Each of us – whoever we are – is enmeshed in a complex web of power relationships. Our life stories will have been deeply affected by, for instance, the educational institutions we attended; the expectations that adults had of us, in turn subtly affected by their learned expectations of people 'like us' (most notably those of our gender, race, and mental and physical ability). Our childhood stories may well include experiences born of our conformity to such expectations, or departure from them – for these can be comfortably rewarding or searingly painful. And this is only the beginning of any human being's encounters with power. To return to Susan Engel one last time, she points out that:

> Most moments of remembering are not done alone in the process of self-understanding or self-contemplation. Many personal recollections that contribute to one's identity unfold in highly motivated and charged situations – where there are other people. You are trying to justify yourself, impress another person, show how you are the same, or different, from others. These situations then end up shaping one's life story as it emerges across time and place. In this way context plays a huge role in determining the self one knows through one's stories about the past.[8]

Context is everything, and power relations form the backdrop to every context. Getting to grips with how external structures of power have profound and deeply personal effects upon us can be achieved only by exploring how they shape our stories; and how we, in choosing how to conceive of and retell our stories, can exercise our agency in the teeth of that power.

The vagaries of power affect the lives of each and every one of us, regardless of our awareness of this. Yet these power structures in which we are forever caught are, in themselves, human-made. While they may feel, much of the time, anonymous and institutional, they are composed of complex human relationships, and can only be transformed, unmade, and remade, by corporate retellings of collective stories. In what follows we shall explore how story can expose the workings of power: how ways of telling our personal stories can effect personal transformations, and how our personal experiences can expose and highlight the way power works at a corporate level, thereby giving us an insight into how macro-level stories might be changed, and our world transformed.

Subverting dominant stories

The smells that surround me are unfamiliar: the polish of parquet flooring, the disinfectant of communal washrooms; and a strange, rubberized anonymity. The sounds are of the hard physical structures of an institution deserted by its human presence – echoing. No one is here to blur the edges, to ease the shock of my transition from 'there' to 'here'. I have arrived early, apparently, before everyone else. It is my first ever conference. I am 17, frightened, in an empty theological college, in an unfamiliar city, not knowing what to expect.

When others do arrive, they are young people from all over the world – a litany of countries I have never visited and assume I probably never will: Haiti, Zimbabwe, South Africa, the Bahamas, Jamaica, Sri Lanka. As the week develops I become aware of many things about the world and myself that I was unaware of before.

Suddenly it is clear that I am a girl, being looked at in ways that I have not been looked at hitherto. I do not know the meaning of the looks, and cannot always interpret the interest and be sure that I have got it right.

I feel young. I thought it was grown-up to come on a week-long summer conference away from home, on my own. Yet alongside others in their mid twenties – some already political and spiritual leaders in their own right, struggling for social change that will enable their survival – I feel like a child, and vulnerable.

I sense that I am the object of someone else's agenda – the leaders, the grown-ups, the organizers. I can tell (though I cannot say how) that there are certain things they hope we will learn; certain insights they hope we will gain. They clearly want the UK participants to be changed by this experience: to learn about the world in a way that will radicalize us. When I make a contribution that fits their hopes – when I clearly 'get it' – they are delighted. I don't think they know that I know.

Despite the unfamiliarity of the place, I come to realize that I am, after all, at home, because I am speaking the dominant language. The others have to work so much harder. While I struggle to interpret cultural signals and body language, at least the words I speak come easily to me. I notice in the others, from time to time, tiredness and frustration, and a tendency among us all to withdraw to the group with which we feel that minimal translation is necessary.

One day, in a small group discussion, I become acutely aware of something else too: a feeling that I have no content to speak of. The others all have stories: of war and conflict; of apartheid; of struggles for education and belief; of oppression and of chronic poverty. By contrast I feel simply ordinary: an empty space, a gap in the proceedings. The 'normal' is a mystery to itself. It cannot see.

Later I see others like me who feel they have no story turning to those who have to partake of theirs. It's as though finding our own is too hard. Let us take on the identity of the other, for it is exotic and exciting and so much more tantalizing to be around (if you excise the suffering, that is). And so I discover that we who do not have a story do have a story. But we have to learn to see it.

Sharing the 'earring story' with my friend Rachel helped me to discern certain assumptions at work in my upbringing that might otherwise have remained unexamined or unnoticed. The process of forming my experience into a story and putting it 'out there' into the public domain (albeit the micro domain of a one-to-one with a trusted friend) enabled me to begin to appreciate the subtleties of the value-system that had shaped me. It also enabled me to see that this value-system had threads and tentacles that spread way beyond my immediate home and family. These were forces alive and at work in an invisible way in the culture that had so far surrounded me. At its worst, this value-system could be characterized as a kind of intellectual snobbery (graduates are somehow 'better than' or more worthy of respect than non-graduates; productivity of the mind is more valuable than manual skills). At its best, it could be construed as a cherishing of the non-material (the world of ideas and beliefs) over and above the world of things and appearances. Sharing my story with Rachel turned it from an ordinary, unremarkable way of being, into something that could have been otherwise, largely because the cultural backdrop against which Rachel had grown up *had been otherwise*. Alone with my experience and my heritage, I had no story; in conversation with Rachel, I could begin to pull out important lessons about my formation as a person, and therefore my identity.

In my experience, the extent to which we feel simply 'normal', or 'ordinary', is the extent to which we feel we have nothing to say about ourselves. We are unremarkable. We have no story. It's at this point that we need to question what is being hidden from us, and why. At the age of 17, in the context of an international conference, I couldn't see (yet) the specificity of my experience. I could comprehend that the life experiences all around me were different from mine, but I could not make the connection between these and my own. I saw and felt, all of a sudden, that my life had been one of security and safety, but I didn't see this as being the result of any choices I had made. My life to date felt pretty much non-negotiable: compulsory free education, good health care on demand, and enough food to eat every day. Yet suddenly, through hearing the stories of others, I knew that it might easily not have been this way. But I couldn't yet see that this was my story, and that it depended on theirs – that I had these things, in part at least, because many of them did not.

So where is the power? The key to answering this question lies in the fact that power cannot always be felt. The paradox of my youth conference story is that a young, unquestionably vulnerable middle-class Western white girl, alone in a strange city for the first time, is also a living repository of the stories and experiences of the collective that has grown her. Though she may feel personally small and insignificant (and I did), she nevertheless manifests the possibilities, potentialities and opportunities that are given to her, regardless of who she is, in an unequal world that works to a system that is designed to benefit people just like her. Being in a powerful position isn't always about having the kind of power that politicians have: that is, the means to determine, in an obvious way, the fate of others. Being powerful can also mean living out of a set of privileges that are unexplored. We cannot understand our identity without understanding systems of privilege and how they work.

Let's take another example in order to make this clear. While I was writing the first chapter of this book, I was simultaneously getting to know a friend who has Asperger's syndrome. This has been described by Tony Attwood, an expert on autistic spectrum disorders, thus:

> I consider that children and adults with Asperger's syndrome have a different, not defective, way of thinking. The person usually has a strong desire to seek knowledge, truth and perfection with a different set of priorities than would be expected with other people. There is also a different perception of situations and sensory experiences. The overriding priority may be to solve a problem rather than satisfy the social or emotional needs of others. The person values being creative rather than co-operative. The person with Asperger's syn-

drome may perceive errors that are not apparent to others, giving considerable attention to detail, rather than noticing the 'big picture'. The person is usually renowned for being direct, speaking their mind and being honest and determined and having a strong sense of social justice. The person may actively seek and enjoy solitude, be a loyal friend and have a distinct sense of humour.[9]

Reading my account in Chapter 2 of what happens when you meet somebody for the first time, my friend, who refers to herself as 'an aspie', offered the following reflection on how this experience feels to her – in particular the negotiation of the assumption that the obvious thing to do is to look someone in the eye and to shake their hand:

A person. Who are they? Any clues? Beard? Glasses? Tall? Clothes? I have some idea whether they're male or female by now. If I've known them for years or they're in context, it's much faster.

Oh my . . . they're facing me and looking at me. Looking at people's eyes is like looking into a 500 watt spotlight. I can't explain why. A hand! Where the heck did that come from? It's moving towards me! Oh . . . I think they want me to shake it. I wonder what they get out of it, since all it does for me is cause painful sensory overload. Think, girl, think! What do we do now? Oh yes, the eye contact. Summon all the calmness you can, and make eye contact (eek!!!) whilst smiling graciously and saying 'How do you do' if you've calculated they're someone formal and new, and something else if they're not. This may go wrong, according to how well I've calculated it. Saying 'Hi mate, how's it going?' to a Bishop may be a Jolly Bad Thing, for example. If in doubt, go for 'Hello'.

I wonder whether I got that right? I'm not sure what they said to me – did they have a name? There is too much else being processed in my mind to focus on it. I guess I'd better now work out what else they're saying and what I'm supposed to say back to them. Maximum concentration on calm cheerfulness and trying to listen intently, which is very important indeed since I really do care about people even if I often find them totally baffling because of the way they choose to communicate.

What's more, in business I have to do this perhaps fifty times in an average networking evening, and cope with everything else that goes on at them. There should be medals.

It's great meeting other aspies. We face into the room, not each other, and just chat.

Not quite the same as what goes through the mind of NT folk. Unless I get it exactly right, they're probably thinking 'What a bl**dy rude person'.[10]

The first thing I learned from this response is that I have an identity about which I knew nothing. I am an 'NT' – 'neurotypical'. In other words, ordinary. The second thing I learned is that in everything I have written, said and done – for my whole life – I have made basic assumptions about the way the human brain works that hold only for the majority of people, not for all people. Now I realize that this assumption has been incorrect. There is a significant minority of people whose brains do not work in the same way as mine. I have assumed a human universal where there is none, including in this book.

It also dawns on me that I am, in this context, a representative of those 'with power'. Because people like me make the rules about social interactions, by virtue of the fact that we are in the majority. And every time we conform to the rules, without question, we reinforce them, thereby making things more difficult for those who do not fit. As a collection of 'normal' individuals, we shape – albeit unknowingly and unintentionally – a set of criteria for appropriate and inappropriate behaviour by which we are all then judged, and some are found wanting. And those who are found wanting in turn feel excluded and devalued. In short, those in the minority – in this case those with Asperger's syndrome – have to fit into the world that we, the majority, create. And they pay the price for playing the game of social interaction by our rules (in anxiety, stress, humiliation and exhaustion). I think back on all the meetings I have convened, workshops I have run, talks I have given, articles I have written, prayers I have said, critiques of the ideas of others that I have offered, and I realize that none of this work takes into account the needs or perspectives of my friend. Again, the 'normal' (the NT) is invisible to itself. The realization, however, is the beginning of change.

Winning the race

When we speak from the position of 'normality', we assume that we are speaking for everyone. So, in the preceding example, I assumed that the methodologies I employed in my work were applicable to everyone, whereas in fact they were primarily designed for people like me – neurotypical people. In his brilliant book, *White*, Richard Dyer exposes the ways in which this works in terms of assumptions about race. He says:

> the position of speaking as a white person is one that white people now almost never acknowledge and this is part of the condition and power of whiteness: white people claim and achieve authority for what they say by not admitting, indeed not realising, that for much of the time they speak only for whiteness.[11]

His aim in writing his book is, he says, 'to come to *see* that position of white authority in order to help undermine it'.[12] His discipline is film studies, and the book explores images of white people in film. As he says,

There has been an enormous amount of analysis of racial imagery in the past decades . . . Yet until recently a notable absence from such work has been the study of images of white people. Indeed, to say that one is interested in race has come to mean that one is interested in any racial imagery other than that of white people. Yet race is not only attributable to people who are not white, nor is imagery of non-white people the only racial imagery.[13]

His perspective is crucial to the analysis we are building about power and human identity for, as he says:

As long as race is something only applied to non-white peoples, as long as white people are not racially seen and named, they/we function as a human norm. Other people are raced, we are just people . . . There is no more powerful position than that of being 'just' human. The claim to power is the claim to speak for the commonality of humanity. Raced people can't do that – they can only speak for their race. But non-raced people can, for they do not represent the interests of a race. The point of seeing the racing of whites is to dislodge them/us from the position of power, with all the inequalities, oppression, privileges and sufferings in its train, dislodging them/us by undercutting the authority with which they/we speak and act in and on the world.[14]

There have been many explorations of the effects of institutional racism upon black and Asian people. Rarely explored are its effects upon those of us who are constructed as 'normal' in this context – i.e. people like Richard Dyer and myself who are white. The Stone Center in the USA has worked to develop 'Relational Cultural Theory' (RCT), that is, to explore the ways in which interpersonal relationships both represent and reproduce cultures in which they are embedded. In a recent collection of their papers entitled *The Complexity of Connection*, Maureen

Walker and Jean Baker Miller focus on racial images, suggesting that:

> In much of the conversation about so-called diversity, we focus on those people who have been socialized as 'less than' and we try to address and understand what we call internalized oppression (meaning how oppressed people begin to believe the false images of themselves that the oppressor group creates). However, there's not much talk about what happens to members of the dominant group. The situation of 'structured in' inequality also distorts the dominant person's sense of who she/he is in the world, whether in the smaller immediate world of friends and family or in the larger society. A person who is socialized to believe that she/he is 'better than' can have a sense of identity that is built on relational images that are malformed and misguided. When we talk about simple diversity, I don't think we get a sense of that. Because this structured inequality is not named most of the time, people in the dominant group end up with problems they don't understand.[15]

Let me be crystal clear at this point. The aim of the current discussion is not to claim that 'white people have problems too', and therefore to claim a slab of the cake of attention for ourselves in the interests of valuing diversity. If Walker and Baker Miller are right that white people have a malformed and misguided sense of our identity, precisely because we have been constructed, through our whiteness, as 'better than' others, then the crucial additional point to note is that we have been *rewarded* through that process, and since we do not want to give up the rewards, we do not want to change. I suggest that a subconscious recognition that we have been thus rewarded is at least partly at the root of our inability to 'see' our specificity. Overcoming racism is an ongoing and ever-present challenge for all humanity, but where we are positioned in the power structures determines the nature of our role in that project. As Walker and Baker Miller put it:

> Typically what we get in much so-called diversity training is that the people who inhabit the more powerful categories need to behave better. That's certainly true. However, relational-cultural healing is also about how everybody needs to be open to movement. The gross and subtle inequalities of a stratified culture inhibit our willingness to receive and to allow and show others that they have an impact on us. We get stuck with these images of the other person or of ourselves that make it hard to move or to be open to any kind of movement.[16]

As the visible and the invisible, the 'storied' and the 'normal', we need to work together to subvert the 'dominant story' that has surrounded us all for centuries, with its myriad and complex manifestations: from religious imagery of good and evil, to the transatlantic slave trade, to political segregation and the disenfranchisement of millions, to discrimination in employment and immigration policies in our own country right now. This is the story that says that white is better than black. And we need to be prepared for the fact that, in the process of subverting that dominant story, we will all end up feeling differently about ourselves, and about one another.

Of his own personal journey towards a recognition of the privileges that are his precisely because of his white identity, Robert Jensen writes, with refreshing honesty:

> Can we accept that many white people have worked hard to accomplish things, and also that those people's accomplishments were made possible in part because they were white in a white supremacist society? Like almost everyone, I have overcome certain hardships in my life. I have worked hard to get where I am, and I work hard to stay there. But

to feel good about myself and my work, I do not have to believe that 'merit' alone, as defined by white people in a white supremacist country, got me here. I can acknowledge that in addition to all that hard work, I got a significant boost from white privilege, which continues to protect me every day of my life from certain hardships. At one time in my life, I would not have been able to say that, because I needed to believe that my success in life was due solely to my individual talent and effort. I saw myself as a heroic American, the rugged individualist. I was so deeply seduced by the culture's mythology that I couldn't see the fear that was binding me to those myths, the fear that maybe I didn't really deserve my success, that maybe luck and privilege had more to do with it than brains and hard work. I was afraid I wasn't heroic or rugged, that I wasn't special.[17]

Dyer concludes, very powerfully:

White power . . . reproduces itself regardless of intention, power differences and goodwill, and overwhelmingly be-cause it is not seen as whiteness, but as normal. White people need to learn to see themselves as white, to see their parti-cularity. In other words, whiteness needs to be made strange.[18]

Being a success

It is noticeable in this exploration of one particular set of power structures – racial ones – that other interlocking and overlapping 'dominant stories' are at work. There are two in particular that I would like to explore further here. It is significant that these emerge above most powerfully in the writings of Robert Jensen, a white man. The first of these stories at work in our culture is an assumption that we should always be 'on the up' (Jensen's vision of 'overcoming hardships in order to be successful'); the second is the related assumption that we all aspire to be autonomous indi-viduals (Jensen's 'rugged individualist').

Cultural studies scholar Jackie Stacey was diagnosed with a rare form of cancer in her early thirties, and wrote her book *Teratologies: A Cultural Study of Cancer* as a result. She writes vividly of the shock of the diagnosis and its impact on her sense of identity:

> In the light of a cancer diagnosis, these new narratives of the body rescript the story of my life with ruthless editorial authority. While the mind has been full of stories of life, the body had been planning another story: the threat of death. How should my life be imagined in such an unexpected context? Can the self be reinvented to cope with the shock? What kind of person does not know they have cancer?[19]

Her sudden transition from being (in my terms) 'normal' to being someone with 'a story' (in this case, someone with a rare cancer diagnosis) exposes to her the hitherto invisible dominant stories that shape our culture, and she is able to write about these in a way that is deeply moving and also politically powerful. Beginning with insights which echo those of Susan Engel earlier in this chapter, she says:

> Stories about illness are an intensification of the way in which we generally understand our lives through narrative. The experience of cancer may bring these narrative processes into particularly sharp focus, but in many ways it only makes explicit the importance of narratives in the construction of self in contemporary culture. We have stories about our childhood, a mixture of our memories and the family favourites we have heard repeatedly. We tell stories about our relationships, both successful and otherwise. We relate our (public and private) stories about who we are and what makes us special or different from the next person . . . When something unexpected occurs, such as illness, the scripts need rewriting, but normally the shock of the

experience can be partly absorbed by the telling of a new story . . .[20]

Crucially for our purposes, however, this leads her to the following insight:

In contemporary Western culture, we are encouraged to think of our lives as coherent stories of success, progress and movement. Loss and failure have their place only as part of a broader picture of ascendance. The steady upward curve is the favoured contour . . . in a society so obsessed with its own progress and improvement it is almost impossible for us to avoid the pull of such narratives. In the face of crisis, another story begins and with the power of retrospection the past is rewritten for the exigencies of the present and the future.[21]

In her work, Stacey brings both an acute awareness and an incisive critique of cultural expectations that would drive her narrative of illness in a particular direction. She explores, from the inside, how it feels to encounter the deep pull to serve our culture's investment in 'success' and 'triumph over tragedy'. And she deliberately resists this pull because she wants to see what it is that our society is hiding from itself. In the process of writing, she lays bare for us the complex and overlapping investments that we have in telling our stories that way. For, she asks,

what remains untold in these heroic narratives? What does linearity exclude? What can not be restored with closure? Where is the continued chaos and disorder in such accounts? Where is the forgotten pain? Stories of progress and rationality are tempting, but perpetuate the illusion of life as a steady upward learning curve in which all crises have a profound meaning.[22]

Futility, mess, meaninglessness, pain and failure. Stacey knows that society is deeply invested in airbrushing out such experiences through the stories we tell ourselves. We prefer, apparently, stories in which these are overcome or banished. Why is that? She provides us with an explanation when she says,

> There are variables beyond our prediction and influences beyond our control that disrupt the easy linearity of the classic triumph-over-tragedy cancer narrative ... I may have wished to write [such] a story at certain moments, and some readers may want to read one (perhaps despite themselves). But I see such projects not only as disappointing to (and even condemning of) the person who does not make it, but also potentially very worrying in terms of the cultural ideals they promise: those fantasies of omnipotence, of masculine invincibility, of individual effect.[23]

Being autonomous

So we are brought to our final theme in this exploration of 'dominant stories' and their political impact. That is, individual autonomy. For futility, mess, meaninglessness, pain and failure have one thing in common. As Stacey suggests, they imply a loss of control. They speak of the chaos and unpredictability that is at the heart of every human life, whether we realize it or not. Needless to say, most of us (by which I mean those of us fortunate enough to have privileges to exercise, whatever those might be) go to great lengths not to realize it. We live in a society that promulgates the primacy of what Stacey calls 'individual effect' – that is, that our fate is entirely in our own hands.

Psychotherapists Dave Mearns and Mick Cooper offer the following helpful summary of the way in which the Western mindset has been formed:

Up until the mid-twentieth century, a particular understanding of human existence came to dominate the western mind. Exemplified in the thinking of the French mathematician and philosopher René Descartes, this 'modern' worldview understands human existence in fundamentally individualistic terms. Here, each human being is conceptualised as a sovereign, autonomous, individual monad, fundamentally distinct and separate from other people around him.[24]

However, they go on to explore how this mind-set has shifted and is shifting:

Are we really so separate from other human beings? Over the course of the twentieth century, many philosophers and psychologists have challenged this assumption: arguing, instead, that we are fundamentally and inextricably intertwined with others, and that our being is first and foremost a 'being-in-relation'. In other words ... that we do not exist as individuals first and then come together with others to form relationships. Rather ... that we exist with others first, and only after that come to develop some notion of individuality or separateness ... And if we conceptualise human existence in this way, other existences become much more central to the essence of who we are. In other words, at the level of lived-being, we are constantly interacting with others, or thinking about others, or imagining doing things with others, or using tools that have emerged from an interpersonal matrix.[25]

We might sum up this shift as being towards an assumption that the 'we' precedes the 'I'. However, in terms of how power structures work in our society, there is little evidence that this shift is having much impact on whom and what we value: quite the opposite. I would agree with the writers from the aforementioned Stone Center when they say:

The dominant (white, male, middle-class, heterosexual) culture valorizes separation. To the extent that relationships are emphasized, they are viewed as primarily utilitarian, as aids to the achievement of a separate self. Our western psychologies focus on individual personality traits, movement toward autonomy, independence, success accomplished through competitive achievement. They underemphasize the importance of connection, growth-fostering relationship, and the need to participate in the growth of relationship and community.[26]

Our conception of ourselves as autonomous individuals can sound like an abstract philosophical issue. But it is not. For there are material power structures at work in the world that ensure that only certain kinds of people have the option of embracing individual autonomy. Privilege is therefore conferred on such people, and they become (according to dynamics we have explored at length in this chapter) the 'normal ones' – the 'powerful ones'. They become the yardstick by which others are judged. So those who are physically and mentally well, who do not have a disability that affects their potential to be economically independent, who are old enough to look after themselves but not so old that they need the support of others, are constructed as 'normal' and therefore exemplary.

Those who are dependent on the physical care of others, on external economic support, or upon the emotional nurturing of carers, friends and family, are – very oddly – seen as exceptional. As a society we are most comfortable when we can see dependence as episodic and temporary – not woven into the very essence of our humanity. We manifest an expectation that when someone falls short of the ideal of autonomy, in whatever way, then something will be done to rectify the situation, and therefore to redeem the person. Those who are irredeemable in this way become society's 'losers'. As the Stone Center authors put it:

In a culture that valorizes separation and autonomy, persons with cultural privilege can falsely appear more self-sufficient and so will be judged as healthier, more mature, more worthy of the privilege the society affords. Those who enjoy less cultural privilege (whether by virtue of race, ethnicity, sexual orientation, or economic status) will more likely be viewed as deficient and needy. They are more likely to be subject to systematic disadvantage and culture shaming.[27]

Their insight here also helps us to see how the various forms of 'better than' ultimately overlap and become part of the same picture. Our society is structured according to a series of 'better thans': rich is better than poor, straight is better than gay, male is better than female, white is better than black, productive is better than unproductive. Set alongside these things the generic 'independent is better than dependent', for instance, and we can see how those with fewer opportunities to make money (because of institutional discrimination which deems them automatically 'less than': women, black people, those with disabilities) are landed with the double burden of being blamed for their consequent potential economic dependence.

We have now seen how overarching 'macro stories' structure our external world, and set in place power structures that have a profound effect on how each of us sees our identity. The macro stories work by making certain things 'normal', invisible and therefore unquestionable. Our personal 'micro stories' and life experiences are always played out in dialogue with the macro stories, but because the latter are invisible, we may not always realize that this is the case. For instance, if my individual story is one of feeling worthless because I am unemployed, I may feel alone in my shame, blame myself for my situation, and begin to apply to myself all kinds of identity categories: hopeless, unsuccessful, a 'loser'. If I remember, however, that there is a powerful macro story at work, telling me that we are each intended to be totally independent and successful people all of the time, I will realize that many of my feelings of worthlessness are caused by this macro story. In other words, once I 'see' this macro story for what it is, I begin to undo its power – to subvert it. I begin to see that it is not simply a neutral statement of fact about the nature of human beings. Rather, it is a particular construction of reality designed to protect the superiority and social positioning of those who benefit from it – i.e. in this case, those who currently have jobs, are economically independent, and are therefore enabled to feel good about being 'better than' those without.

However, subverting the macro story by 'seeing' it for what it is takes us only so far towards social transformation. It helps us to value our identities as individuals, but it doesn't reshape the power structures. We need to find ways of deploying our micro stories in order to reshape the macro ones. That is our next area of exploration.

Telling untold stories

I think I am feeling an absence of an absence, and I'm wondering how I can tell.

I am walking with you in the hills. We are holding hands. This feels deeply unsettling to me, for you are a man, and I am a woman and this is not what I am used to. Nobody looks away when they catch sight of us. No one averts their gaze. I expect to feel relief but I do not. This newfound sense of security has a paradoxical effect. I feel destabilized, cut adrift from my old identity, even as I am rescued from the sense of dislocation it brought with it. The social kaleidoscope has twisted; the pieces have fallen into myriad new places all around me, and I am located differently now.

I am angry that in another year, with a former lover, on a similar walk, in the same hills, if I dared to hold hands with her, even to let go when others came near, I was looked at differently. Not with hostility so much as a blank emptiness.

With a weight behind the void – a sense of knowing who was in charge, and it wasn't us. A deep awareness that however self-confident we were, their tolerance could be withdrawn at any moment – if it was there in the first place.

Now, it seems, I am legitimized – worthy of recognition. It is so subtle that I wonder at the enormity of its effects; so slight that I doubt myself and my perceptions. To the extent that others are 'normal' they will doubt them too. Am I simply imagining this? Yet these fractional changes feel like the difference between belonging and not; between being a person and less than a person. Those I am meeting on narrow pathways in these wooded and fertile hills reflect something of me in their eyes as they meet mine. In their sense of recognition I experience estrangement. 'You are one of us,' they seem to say. I do not want to be.

From the inside, I am the same person on the same walk in the same hills – whoever I am with. Holding hands or not. And it is suddenly clear to me how the variegated and nuanced, complex and beautiful, multiple inflections of my personhood have been forced by the world into a blunt and dichotomous either/or. I will not choose.

Stigmatized identities

In a chapter entitled 'Monsters', Jackie Stacey reflects on a perhaps unexpected insight gained from her experience of cancer treat-ment. She notices how difficult the nursing staff find it to utter 'the C word'. She describes the twice daily exchange as one shift hands over to another. One nurse introduces her to her colleague, but instead of saying her name ('this is Jackie') followed by her illness (cancer), the nurse says her name, then merely gives an awkward smile.

The most interesting thing about this experience, however, is not simply the stigma that still surrounds the disease of cancer, but the link she makes with another aspect of her identity:

My experience of the cancer diagnosis and its aftermath felt very familiar. I had definitely been here before. Although the context and the content were different, many of the rules were the same. Certain feelings fitted emotional and bodily memories that I recognised: the ways in which other people's fears were condensed in particular kinds of language practices and behaviour rituals.[28]

She goes on:

The prohibition on speaking the C word reminded me of my experience of the L word. Albeit for very different reasons, I have always been struck by the depth of people's anxieties about saying the word 'lesbian'. The censorship and self-censorship which operate around this cultural category prohibit speaking it aloud, especially in public places . . . When, and if, the silence is broken, all kinds of euphemisms are used to speak about these categories without saying the L word or the C word. In the case of deviant sexualities euphemisms are commonplace . . . Cancer, too, is spoken about through euphemism.[29]

Stacey therefore uses her experience of cancer to shine a sharper spotlight on her experience of being a lesbian. It is my experience too that living out a stigmatized lesbian identity can feel like living as an absence, or a partial absence. One has an acute and constant awareness that those around may be feeling anxious and uncomfortable with who you are, a feeling that is reinforced by the huge effort they deploy to avoid reference to or mention of it. This, albeit usually very polite evasion (mine is, after all, a middle-class experience) leaves one feeling erased from the social map. It makes clear that one is included only under very restricted conditions. Even to test the nature of those restrictions is to risk painful or humiliating rejection. As Stacey puts it:

Part of the feeling that we belong to a culture occurs in the moments when . . . recognition bestows a legitimate sense of place on us. When no such place appears on the horizon, even as a distant promise, its absence marks the subject as other, as outsider, as alone. This surfaces . . . through the repeated negotiations of the responses of others. Once (or if) the stigmatised category has been named, it has to be continually reiterated as the lesbian 'comes out' (if she decides to) and the person with cancer 'breaks the news' to friends, family and colleagues . . . And through their shocked reaction your own sense of discrepancy between who-you-were and who-you-must-be-now is repeatedly rehearsed.[30]

Naming and labelling

In the case of sexuality, what Stacey calls the dialogue between 'who you were' and 'who you must be now' is a conversation between the way one names oneself, and the ways in which one is labelled by others. It is the power struggle between the weight of the 'normal' (the exemplary, the heterosexual) and the 'micro story' of one's own feelings and relational history. It is no wonder that 'coming out' is so frightening, entailing as it does the need for us to wait upon the reactions of others to our self-naming – making ourselves vulnerable to all manner of misnamings and misunderstandings.

Frightening it may be, but such 'coming out' has proved to be a hugely powerful tool in achieving social transformation. It is through the conscious and repeated acts of coming out, by thousands of people in same-sex relationships, in a variety of contexts (at work, in families, in churches), that our culture has undergone a massive shift in its attitudes towards lesbian and gay sexuality over the past 20 years. The single, derogated, criminalized and pathologized category of 'the homosexual' has gone. Taking its place is a vibrant, diverse and politically powerful community that currently chooses to call itself the LGBT community (lesbian, gay, bisexual and transgender). It will, I am sure, evolve other names for itself as the complexity of personal experiences that constitute it, and the alliances and friendships that are at its heart, continue to change and develop, and to unearth new depths of human experience that have been hidden from us thus far.

'Coming out' has provided a framework for many individuals to tell the story of who they are, on their own terms. The phrase originates in the arena of sexual identity, but it is now used in connection with other aspects of personal identity too. It is a way of giving voice to our own experiences but also, crucially, of making links with those who share them in order to establish networks of solidarity, support, and sometimes of advocacy and political change-making too.

Feminist analyses of sexual violence, for instance, developed over the last 20 or so years, have been built upon the encourage-ment to women to 'speak out' about experiences that they have hitherto been unable to discuss with others. These include inci-dences of rape, sexual harassment and sexual assault as adults; sexual abuse as children, including incestuous abuse – and abuse by other figures in authority: priests, doctors and counsellors. Bell hooks sums up for us why speaking out is so important when she says, 'Coming to voice is an act of resistance. Speaking becomes both a way to engage in active self-transformation and a rite of passage where one moves from being object to subject. Only as subjects can we speak. As objects, we remain voiceless – our beginnings defined and interpreted by others.'[31] The motiva-tions for 'breaking the silence' about sexual violence are there-fore variable: the curtailment of personal isolation, exposure of oppressors and wrong-doers, the validation of experience, per-sonal empowerment, and public education. A corpus of feminist literature has developed that encompasses the telling of sur-vivors' stories; empirical work on the nature and incidence of various forms of sexual violence, and feminist analysis of both kinds of evidence.

The complexity of naming oneself

There is, however, a delicate path to be trodden in this world of 'breaking the silence', 'coming out', and giving voice to one's personal experience. Precisely because of the potential political potency of such moves, we are returned to where we began this chapter – with the insight that stories are not, in themselves, 'innocent'. Political purposes hover in the background as we decide how to tell our stories: what to include and what to leave out. Stories are never told raw or whole – but always in a particular context. And the encouragement to tell one's story in a certain way in order to help bring about particular forms of social transformation can – sometimes inadvertently – contribute to the setting up of new cycles of marginalization.

An example might help. In the early days of the gay liberation movement, the argument for decriminalization was that homosexuality was simply a trait that a small minority of men (the law bothered itself only with men) were born with, and it was unchangeable. Since those who discovered themselves to be homosexual had no choice about being otherwise, and since life was so hideous for them anyway, the assertion was that there was no danger in decriminalization, because there was no way it was going to lead to more men embracing a homosexual lifestyle.

The pressure, therefore, was to tell 'coming out' stories that reinforced this political message. To a certain extent, these became formulaic – with common features such as the early age at which men discovered their homosexuality; the fact that this discovery was always traumatic and dreadful; the notion that their identity was felt to be irrevocable. And the stories that were given the highest profiles were those from men who – aside from their sexuality – were in dominant social categories (that is, white, affluent and well-educated). Again, the political reasons for this were clear – to persuade law-makers (white, affluent and well-educated) that in all other respects, homosexuals were just like them – not the scary 'other', out to undermine their value-system and notions of civilization. This dynamic was reflected in discussions about homosexuality within the Christian community too. The point was made that since homosexuality could not be 'helped', it must be part of God's created order, and therefore those for whom same-sex attraction was unavoidable should be treated with sympathy and respect, not met with stigmatization and rejection. Again, however, it was the stories of those already powerful within the church structures – homosexual clergy – that dominated, and that became the focus for discussion in the media and elsewhere.

Within this political context, it became very difficult for stories to be voiced that did not fit the strictures set by the demands of realpolitik. Women's experience of same-sex attraction and desire was nowhere in the picture. Many, for instance, embraced a lesbian identity after being married and raising children and did not necessarily believe that they had been lesbian all along without realizing it (as the 'born that way' script demanded). There was no space for stories in which women and men chose to be lesbian and gay. Men who got married, had kids, and only later really embraced their gay sexuality were also politically inconvenient. Women and men for whom gender was simply not the determining factor in sexual attraction were exhorted to make their minds up and come down on one side or the other of the rapidly congealing gay/straight divide. As the gay liberation movement developed, therefore, there were undoubtedly many who felt that their story did not fit the necessary (because politically expedient) story, and who therefore felt isolated and alone.

Gradually, however, the movement evolved. It did find ways of hearing the inconvenient stories, and found ways of integrating and incorporating them into its vision for social transformation. First it discovered that it had ignored women's stories and became the 'lesbian and gay movement' rather than the 'gay movement'. Then it realized that it had unhelpfully reinforced the homo/heterosexual dichotomy, and embraced bisexuality too. Finally, the link between a dichotomous view of sexuality and a dichotomous view of gender, and how one reinforces the other, was recognized through listening to the stories of transgender people. Thus the movement is now termed 'LGBT'. The 'better than' structures that inform the dominant society have undoubtedly had an impact on those of minority sexualities and the communities we have formed. Lesbians will cite many examples of sexist attitudes; gay people of minority ethnic backgrounds will give plenty of examples of racism; older gay men constantly encounter what they call 'body fascism' that values youthfulness above old age – a trend that also has an impact on those with disabilities. However, that said, there has clearly been an evolution in this political movement away from simply focusing on and hearing the stories of a narrow group of privileged men, towards building a diverse community, embracing the rainbow flag in a conscious attempt to value difference. And so the vision for social transformation has got steadily bigger. The umbrella term being the 'queer agenda' – that is (in brief), a healthy and rigorous challenge to any concept of 'normality' that would have us assume that biological sex leads to a certain set of expected gendered behaviours, including the assumption that one must choose a life partner of the so-called 'opposite' sex.

This foray into sexual politics has shown, I hope, that telling our personal stories can have hugely positive effects in terms of what bell hooks calls the 'move from being object to subject'. It can alleviate feelings of isolation, and give us a new voice and a sense of belonging to a community or movement of those who share important aspects of our experience. In this way, story-telling can be the key to social change. We have also seen, however, that the political demands of such change can in turn restrict the nature and diversity of the stories that can be told in public spaces.

How to belong

While we are building our analysis of how the macro story of power works – how the 'normal' is established and rendered invisible – we are quite rightly most interested in the *commonalities* between the micro stories of those who come off badly in the process. If, for instance, we want to understand the dynamics of childhood sexual abuse, we do well to listen to as many stories as possible from children who have had that experience. By drawing out what the stories have in common, we can hopefully begin to figure out what it is about the power of adults that fosters a world where such abuse can thrive. However, our explorations thus far have led us to conclude that we simultaneously need to pay attention to the stories that don't fit as we build our analysis. It is tempting to squash and to silence these, as we have seen, because strategies for change require coherence and consistency. Not only does this mean that certain stories become marginalized yet again – at great cost to those concerned – there is also a danger of forming rigid boundaries around identity categories that become static. This brings us, finally, to an exploration of the tensions at the heart of belonging.

Another example might help us – this time from the arena of gender politics. Within the feminist movement of the 1980s and 1990s there was much discussion about the need for 'women only' spaces. Some people (myself included) were in favour of occasional spaces where women could explore the challenges (many and varied) of flourishing in a society that seemed to be designed to fit men's experience, not ours. We sometimes used the word 'safe' to describe what a space felt like when it was shared only by other women. Other people (including many men) argued that there was no need for such spaces – even that they were counter-productive. They took the view that social change would never happen if the most important discussions happened in 'women-only ghettoes' (they called them ghettoes, we called them spaces) so that those who most needed to change (i.e. men) had no access to the insights so generated (suddenly they really wanted to change!). The obvious response to this was that the occasional women-only discussion did not alter the fact that there were plenty of mixed spaces left in which such learning might take place, and that perhaps the stories enunciated in places where women actually got some air-space (proven not to be the case, on the whole, in mixed company) might as a result be more effectively communicated.

A third perspective was rather more extreme and became known as 'separatist'. This group felt that the safety experienced in women-only spaces should be the rule rather than the exception, and set about organizing their lives in such a way that they had as little contact as possible with men, masculinity and patriarchal value-systems. 'Sleeping with the enemy' was obviously a problem, so many separatist feminists embraced so-called 'political lesbianism' and lived in women-only households. Others learned to take on roles previously ascribed to men – so women became plumbers, painters and decorators, builders and gardeners (so that men would not need to be brought in to mend stuff). Another aim was to raise children in contexts free from the influence of men. Some feminist separatists even explored, apocryphally, new ways of referring to themselves, using 'wimmin' or 'womyn', in order to escape the fate of having 'man' and 'men' at the heart of their self-naming.

As one who happily claimed (and still claims) the designation 'feminist', and who embraced the opportunities afforded by women-only spaces, I would argue that there was much that was positive about them – especially within the terms of our current discussion. Conversations in women-only spaces were of a different quality and depth; they enabled us to articulate the questions at the heart of our struggles to be the best that we could be – and to discover that our self-doubts and (often) under-confidence had a social origin and were not simply born of individual weakness. This analysis enabled us to work out strategies for building our confidence and increasing our assertiveness, and often to think bigger about our visions and aims in life, and our fitness to embrace them. In other words, the macro story of sexism and patriarchy was exposed to us and made visible through our sharing of our micro stories of how it felt to live in its shadow. Women began to see ourselves differently, and attempted to change society for the better.

However, it is also my view that something unfortunate happened at the moment when a wish for permanent separatism took hold, and there were three particular debates that ignited my personal sense of unease. First, there was the question of the place of boy children in women-only households. An assumption seemed to abound that boys needed to be saved from their maleness, and that this would happen if they were brought up 'correctly' (i.e. in a counter-cultural, anti-sexist way). This seemed to me vaguely ridiculous and certainly sinister. Second, male-to-female transsexuals expressed a desire to be part of women-only households and groupings, setting off a frenzy of controversy as to whether such women were the same as those who had been born women. The way in which this was debated came dangerously close to assessing people as to their 'authentic' status as women. Were these 'proper' or 'real' women? Often such transsexuals were banned from women-only spaces on the grounds that most of their lived experience had been as men, and that this made them different. The third challenge came from black women, some of whom questioned the legitimacy of separatism by pointing out that for them, racism was at least as damaging to their personhood as sexism, and that in working against racism, they both needed and wanted to stand shoulder to shoulder with black men. For them, therefore, separatism was not an option. This exposed clearly how a movement that had grown out of an attempt to expose the oppression of one group by another (oppression of women by men), had – inadvertently or not, depending on your perspective – ended up promoting oppression – this time of black women by white women. Why? Because, through dynamics such as those explained so clearly by Richard Dyer earlier in this exploration of power, certain women had assumed it was possible to speak for all women, when in fact it was not.

These various discussions and dynamics gave me, rightly or wrongly, an uneasy sense that an ideology was getting in the way of humanity. Like Jackie Stacey making the links between the L word and the C word, my own realization was that I had seen a picture like this before – for me, it was in the world of religion. It was called fundamentalism. A way of life was being advocated that involved cutting oneself off from contaminating influences, and building an ideologically correct world within the world as a way of surviving. After a while I began to experience a sense of shrinkage of my internal emotional world. I had a sense of myself closing down rather than opening up; of saying 'no' to life rather than embracing its possibilities and taking the risks of saying 'yes'. There was too much internal policing and too many restrictions. I found myself prejudging others according to their gender, and tailoring my expectations of them according to their gender too. I felt that my self-definition as a woman was formed over and against the definition of men as 'other'. In short, I began to find that the joys of discovering the empowerment of commonality can easily tip over into embracing a static and rigid identity category that inhibits growth and change. I am not saying that this happened to any and every feminist, I am saying that it happened to me, and I know that I am not the only one who felt this way.

All this has left me with a sense that belonging should be embraced wholeheartedly, but also with great caution and a critical edge that must never be abandoned. It is only our self-knowledge that will tell us when we are experiencing legitimate empowerment through our sense of belonging, and when this has tipped over into a narrow and dangerous defensiveness and self-protection. That, I think, is the challenge of identity: how to have a sense of ourselves that is strong and deep enough to enable us to change, but not so strong that it becomes rigid, restricting the directions in which we can grow.

4

Faith

The story of faith

This house of God is cold.

My presence is by force of professional obligation. It is the only thing that brings me here. A deep chill of ambivalence from within meets an unwelcoming frigidity from without. I am run through with trembling. I sit in the presence of a merciless reminder that my soul is restless with yearning for belonging, but I cannot find it here.

And the memory of the Word echoes with a threat, 'She who does not gather with me scatters.'

I am scattered. Faith is strewn before me, but it is not mine. This house of God was once inhabitable, even beautiful. I could love and live its story. What happened? Did I lose something, or was it lost to me? Am I guilty? Is there anything I can do? Now my desires are impaled in their fragility by that which was once their meaning.

And the memory of the Word echoes without hope, 'Once the salt has lost its taste, how can its saltiness be restored?'

I regard the walls of stone that surround me. Their bulk and scale are impressive, as is their claim to protection and security. Yet I experience them as purveyors of magnificent indifference, making everything small. My heart beats as an irrelevance in a cavity of monstrous silence.

And I notice that nothing enters here and remains itself.

Warm air must become cool; light must be filtered and stained; the sun's rays must be refracted and set on new trajectories. Sounds from outside are hushed and suppressed. Only sounds from within are lengthened, enhanced, multiplied and glorified. There is power here, and I am afraid.

Yet the memory of the Word echoes with a promise, 'I have called you by name, you are mine.'

Margaret is 85 years old. She is contemplating the end of her life. She is facing it with a deeply spiritual sensibility: remembering those who have been important to her; reflecting on her relationships with those around her; reminiscing and putting the bits in place; making sense of her story. But she has no spiritual support in that. She feels alone. She was brought up as a Christian and, like many of her generation, churchgoing was part of life. Until one day, 20 years ago, when a church leader said to her, 'If you can't stand up and say every word of the Creed and mean it, you should not call yourself a Christian.' Margaret had frequently had questions and doubts about many aspects of the Christian faith, including parts of the Creed. She had rarely had the opportunity to vocalize them. This comment from an authoritative clergyperson had such a devastating impact upon her that she hasn't been to church since. She feels now that she does not deserve to claim a Christian identity – that her doubts disqualify her. So she is exiled from her faith community at precisely the time when she needs its resources most acutely – as she assesses the meaning of her life, and explores her hopes and fears about what lies ahead for her.

In her alienation from church, Margaret is not alone among those of her age group. Indeed, there are many across all generations who feel ambivalent and confused about their religious identity, and faith is a context where the tensions at the heart of belonging are very acutely felt. Some have a faith identity as part of their personal cultural heritage, but are not quite sure what it means to continue to claim that identity now – particularly if they have fallen away from expressing that faith through conventional means (as in the case of so-called 'lapsed Catholics' and 'secular' Jews and Muslims, for instance). Others have a strong religious belief but feel excluded from the institutions associated with it – often because of personal experiences and ethical choices. Gay and lesbian Christians, for instance, may justifiably feel that the powers-that-be in most Christian denominations would prefer that they did not exist, even if they themselves remain convinced that God loves and accepts them. Catholic women who have needed to undergo abortions or a divorce live with the spectre of the disapproval of the celibate clerical hierarchy. Survivors of sexual abuse and domestic violence may find little understanding within their faith communities of the significance of their experience and what it means for them psychologically and spiritually, and are often left alienated as a result. Sometimes this alienation is reinforced because the ways in which their religious beliefs are affected and changed by such traumatic life experiences seem to be unspeakable in a context of an apparently unquestionable 'received tradition'. Others have a deep sense of personal spirituality – a sense of awe and wonder at the natural world and human relationships – but have no history of engagement with a religious tradition, and can find no communal setting through which such deep feelings can be expressed. There is nowhere to 'belong'. All these examples highlight for us a clutch of important questions at the heart of faith identity.

We could, of course, dismiss Margaret's story – and the many other such stories hinted at above – as having little significance beyond her individual experience. We could say that she has simply misunderstood the nature of credal statements, and placed too much authority in the hands of one religious leader. In that sense, her alienation is her own fault. But such an approach misses a very important point that emerged in our earlier explorations of power and how it works within the context of identity-building. For, in the presence of so many challenging micro stories, we do well to ask ourselves: what is the dominant, and therefore invisible, macro story? What are the hidden assumptions about faith identity that Margaret and so many others collide with so painfully through their personal experience?

At work in Margaret's story is an assumption that faith rests on a self-evident and given corpus of teaching and that this cannot be contested. You take it or leave it. If you take it, you become an adherent of that faith, and if you leave it, you do not. In what follows, I shall refer to that corpus of teaching, in convenient shorthand, as 'doctrine'. For Margaret, this doctrine comes in the form of the Creed. A second assumption is that in order to claim a faith identity one must 'believe', and belief is primarily a matter of individual intellectual assent to the doctrine. Verbalizing this intellectual assent (e.g. through saying the Creed aloud in a public setting) is a way of making one's personal beliefs accessible to, and testable by, others. In Margaret's case, her integrity demands that she not speak aloud things which she is unsure of within herself, for that would seem to her like lying or hypocrisy. A final important assumption is that participation in a faith community is the natural and necessary expression of belief in the doctrine. Its purpose is to reinforce the belief, and this reinforcement comes from surrounding oneself with people who have made a similar, individual, intellectual assent to the same set of doctrines. The strength of the faith community is said to lie in the commonality between its adherents. Margaret's perception is that her doubts disqualify her because they undermine the community by eroding that commonality.

What does it mean, then, to claim the identity, 'Christian'? In both the Church and the secular world, this seems to be a straightforward question with a straightforward answer. You are either a Christian or you are not, and your personally held beliefs form the criteria by which you decide. When my hairdresser asks me, 'Are you a Christian?', she means (and I know because I have asked her), 'Do you believe in God, Jesus and the Bible?' The language used within the Christian community is not a million miles away from my hairdresser's: we 'come to faith', and once this has happened, our task is to shore it up, protect and reinforce it – to keep, develop and nurture it. To the extent that we succeed in this, we remain faithful, and we may share our faith with others. But to the extent that we fail, we 'lose' it. Faith is gained and lost, and whichever happens is down to us. Particular human actions lead to particular outcomes. For example, if you don't embrace the right kind of religious expression, such as going to church, reading the Bible and praying, then your faith identity is in peril.

We are beginning to uncover, then, some characteristics of the 'dominant story' about faith. These are not often visible to those for whom a sense of Christian belonging is easy. It's these assumptions about faith identity that come into play when Christians say, for instance, that people with learning disabilities should not be 'allowed' to participate fully in the Eucharist, because they 'do not know what they are doing'. 'Knowing' is used here in a cognitive way – it is the much over-valued individual intellectual assent at the heart of belief. The assumptions are there again when Christians put up posters declaring, 'If God seems far away – who moved?' – as though a felt sense of God's presence can be conjured up through self-discipline and human will alone. And they are manifest when people declare that 'you cannot really be a Christian if you don't go to church'. Apart from the fact that such things are often said with no appreciation of or interest in why people find church difficult, the underlying rationale is that certain forms of expression must, of necessity, flow from certain beliefs.

In short, the dominant story about faith identity enmeshes us in a vicious triangle where doctrine, belief and expression are inextricably linked together, and have a linear connection. My use of the word 'vicious' stems from an awareness of the acute spiritual pain that can be felt when one finds oneself impaled on any of the three points of this triangle or, indeed, caught up in questions about how the three relate to one another. These experiences can feel like a strangulation of faith, and can leave one feeling a profound sense of alienation from one's spiritual roots. The next step, then, must be to break into this cycle, break open the constituent parts and see whether a better account of faith identity – one that honours the micro stories of those chewed up by the dominant one – is possible.

Doctrine is not innocent

I am using the word 'doctrine' with a deliberate lack of technical theological precision. I use it simply to denote the content of a religious belief-system and, more particularly, those aspects of it that are considered to be non-negotiable for a believer. Within Christianity the non-negotiable varies enormously from tradition to tradition. Some churches and Christian organizations attempt to define it (e.g. you must believe that Jesus is the Son of God; you must believe in the literal truth of the Bible); others do not. Where definitions are set, debate simply shifts from content to interpretation (e.g. what do we mean by 'Son of God'? what constitutes a literal interpretation of the Bible?). In the main, accepted and expected beliefs are rarely definable or transparent. You discover what they are by transgressing them. I am therefore interested not so much in the content of this category of 'doctrine', but in how it functions, and how power is implicated in that process.

Let's explore this through one particular example of an accepted and expected belief among Christians – that one will happily consider oneself a 'servant of all'. This is a particularly powerful and popular notion among clergy as a model of good leadership, based on Jesus' declaration that 'I am among you as one who serves'. On noticing its potency recently, I began also to perceive that it was being used as though it were a neutral model that could be embraced in the same way by anybody and everybody, regardless of their background and status. Because this made me feel distinctly uncomfortable, I wrote the following short article, entitled 'Drudgery or Freedom',[1] to find out whether I was the only one with such ambivalent feelings. Interestingly, the article (published in a diocesan newspaper) elicited an unusually high number of comments for an article of this kind. I will quote the article in full, followed by excerpts from four of the responses. Interestingly, all the respondents were women.

Am I alone in my struggle with servant imagery in relation to Christian discipleship and leadership?

The images in my head are forbidding: young Irish girls doing hard labour in the Magdalen Laundries jostle with the 'Upstairs, Downstairs' world of women and men kept in lowly estate, doffing their caps and touching their forelocks to aristocracies past and present. Then there are the black people in colonial (and many other) contexts, enlisted to cook, clean, scrub, polish, and wet-nurse for wealthy whites. Indeed, inequality seems to be inherent in the concept. Servanthood is about those with less economic and social power carrying out menial (and often unpleasant) tasks on behalf of those with more.

And if the force of the image is in 'reversals' (i.e. those with more power voluntarily renouncing it), then I am haunted by the observation that in ecclesiastical contexts serving God is often confused with serving 'the Church' or (even worse) serving those in authority or of higher status within it, and for this reason it is often those with the least power to renounce, who renounce it first and most convincingly, thus reinforcing their subjugation.

And finally, there's the drudgery. I observe Christian models of servanthood implicated in many forms of ecclesiastical burnout: that of lay people who feel unable to say 'no' when yet another task is allotted; that of clergy (including bishops) who work twelve hours or more a day, seven days a week (or even 'just' six) because they feel a duty to serve, at whatever cost to their health.

So I am in search of redemption for servanthood before I can embrace it. Working on this, I ask myself, 'when am I happy to serve?' One answer comes to me immediately: when I am engaged in artistic and creative endeavour. Call it what you like – the 'muse', 'inspiration', the 'creative force', but when it comes it is like a transcendent presence, speaking through you. You embrace it with joy and follow where it leads because it works in a way that leaves you feeling enlivened, energized and fulfilled. There is no depletion (though there is tiredness). You are expanded, not made small. Serving it is like receiving a gift from beyond, and the response is, indeed, perfect freedom.

So I conclude that the only kind of servant I want to be, and the only kinds of servants I want to serve with, are co-workers: equals who are friends of a mysterious and graceful process that is beyond the understanding of us all and larger than we are, through which we come into our own.

Here are four responses:[2]

I think we are actually, as Christians, stuck with the servant image: Christ washed his disciples' feet to illustrate this kind of service. What I mean is, we are stuck with having to follow the example of adopting an attitude that we are never too great a person, in ourselves, to do something caring for somebody else. That is 'love' in the Christian context. Yes the concept of service has been exploited and abused, but that does not make it a wrong thing to serve others. It will always be a wrong thing to force others to serve and that is the problem we have to address.

Alison is not alone in a struggle with servant imagery. What does it mean for me as a woman who is a priest to be a servant leader given the background, and continuing situation of women predominantly taking on a variety of servant roles? In her book *Living on the Edge* Penny Jamieson (the first woman in the Anglican Communion to become a diocesan bishop in Dunedin, New Zealand) talks of the need for women to recover, and redeem for themselves, a theology of power. Service can be sometimes a more acceptable way into leadership for women for the wrong reasons, and can be a cover for feelings of worthlessness. She says: 'It is only after a woman has both claimed and rejoiced in all she is meant to have and to be that she is free to "give" herself appropriately and to serve the needs of others and not her own needs badly disguised.' To which I can only say a loud AMEN because that is exactly the issue for me.

Please tell Alison Webster, that I'm afraid she's got to put up with servant imagery, whether it makes her happy or not. Jesus started it for Christians, following Isaiah and other writers.

Having just returned from the Bishop's Advisory Panel and having been selected for training for ordination, Alison's article on Drudgery or Freedom really hit home. I have during the past year been praying the prayer of St. Augustine, 'O God, our true life, to know you is life, to serve you is perfect freedom, to enjoy you is a kingdom, and to praise you is the joy and happiness of the soul.' I was aware within my own calling that I have been given a gift, although it seems like a paradox as God has called me to non-stipendiary ministry. But what of my other job? I work in Marks and Spencer's and am an assistant in the espresso bar, a job that involves serving customers all day and, yes, I absolutely love it. But shop work is not treated as a skilled career, it is often low paid and long hours and many workers are not treated well by members of the public or those who employ them. On the last day of work before the Panel, the team I work with told me to stay on the dishwasher for the day, as I was really no use to anyone, nerves were getting the better of me. The dishwasher for me was a retreat day; I stepped back from the customer-focused side of my work and went backstage. This is what I will take into my ministry; clergy have to step back in prayer to dwell with God, to be able to walk in that freedom that God gives us . . . So I pray that all Christians may serve Christ in perfect freedom, by serving, listening and talking to others as equals.

'Drudgery or Freedom' was an attempt to problematize, in a provocative way, the notion that Christian teaching is neutral and objective. Doctrine is always somebody's doctrine. Indeed, we could say that doctrine is just a snapshot of where the beliefs of a community are at a particular point in history. Or, more accurately, they are a snapshot of where the beliefs of the most powerful, articulate and literate members of a faith community are at a particular point in history. They have the wherewithal to define the beliefs of the rest of us, and powerful institutions through which to police the boundaries that they set. The second response to my article highlights one particular aspect of institutional power – that which derives from gender. The priest focuses, in her response, upon the assumption that religious leaders need servant imagery as a corrective to their tendency to think too much of themselves. She shows how, in general terms, women leaders have needed to reclaim a sense of their power, not to downplay it. In societies that have been traditionally male-dominated, the problem for women has been the social construction of ourselves as 'not good enough', which means that our needs as leaders are quite distinct from men's needs.

Belief is always somebody's belief

If it is true that doctrine is always somebody's doctrine, it is also true that belief is always somebody's belief. Who we are is crucial to how and what we believe. Let us return for a moment to our opening story, and the notion, so problematic for Margaret, that faith rests on a self-evident and given corpus of teaching that cannot be contested. In this context it is interesting to note that the other three responses to 'Drudgery and Freedom' all address the perceived 'givenness' of notions of servanthood. Response three is the most uncompromising. Teaching about servanthood must just be accepted as it is, and if it doesn't make sense in the light of personal experience (or if it doesn't 'make you happy'!), you simply have to put up with it. The first response is more pragmatic, though somewhat joyless and grudging: the givens are considered to be, by definition, benevolent. Any negativity must have its origin in our human interpretation of them. In this woman's analysis it is human abuse, misuse and misunderstanding that are at the heart of the problem. The fourth response is unusual in that the ordinand brings to bear a real experience of serving others, in a day-job role that attracts little by way of financial reward or public recognition, and reflects theologically upon that experience, drawing out insights about where servant leadership might lead if embraced in a practical, rather than simply theoretical way. In a sense, she redeems the concept in precisely the way I was suggesting – making equality its focus.

Nobody – as far as I know – ever went to the stake for a heretical interpretation of the meaning of servanthood. But this makes the example all the more useful, for it highlights how, even with such a 'mild' issue, the dynamics of the macro story we have already explored come into play. That is, an invisible assumption is made that there is a correct teaching about servanthood, and that it is our job as Christians to discover what that is, and to align ourselves with it (that is, to 'believe in' it), and then to express that belief in appropriate actions. What also emerges, interestingly, is the way in which the boundaries of belief are simultaneously defended and challenged. Note that it is a fellow lay woman who suggests that I should be 'told' what is non-negotiable in Christianity. She assumes that the boundaries are fixed, but also that it is somebody else's job to police them ('will somebody please tell . . .'), presumably someone with greater spiritual authority than she thinks she has.

Within faith communities we often do not see that belief is always somebody's belief. Rather, we assume that everybody is called to believe the same things in the same way, irrespective of their personal experience, needs and gifts. In this way teachings about how we should and shouldn't be, and what we should and should not think and feel, become the invisible cultural wallpaper against which faith institutions operate. They become part of Christian doctrine (in my loose sense of the term) through no deliberate effort by anyone in particular – but through repeated preaching and teaching by those in positions of power who think we speak for everyone, when really we are expressing what is appropriate and meaningful only for us. So the lack of critical self-awareness among those of us in positions of power ultimately creates doctrines that are hard to accept, and hard to challenge, by those who are more vulnerable.

Looking at faith another way

The tide is low, mist distant. I walk in the shifting space where sea seduces sand.

Here is a place where nothing is clear.

Sky expands above and around me, gently vibrant with hidden winter light. The sea is strangely still. Tiny corrugations shiver then merge to shining smoothness, holding a swell of promise. An isolated wave smiles a transient greeting – instant valediction.

It is not clear where sea becomes sky. No horizon cleaves one realm from another. No line marks the division. There is just an ethereal zone of slow transformation.

It is not clear where sky becomes land. Spectral half-forms emerge, darkened, from yellow-grey luminosity. Their solidity is an assumption.

It is not clear which mirrored wetness is deep pool, which merely mirage on washed sand.

I walk.

I look up at the cliffs. No ageless bulwarks of protection, these. They are yielding, vulnerable, ever-changed by wind, rain and relentless tides. Friable, their lives hang in the

balance as water permeates and land slips, redrawing the
edge of identity.

A chaos of rocks interrupts – colours echoing the honeyed
cliffs, but shapes inhospitable and rejecting.

Here and there white chalk breaks through sand like a
memory. Its quest long-forgotten, it submits, resigned to a
life so long it envies the cliffs' fragility.

I walk.

I wonder – is the tide coming in, or going out? The ground
I am covering with each compacting step, does it signal gain
or loss? Is this liminal space yet to be claimed by the long,
slow stroke of the waves, or has it been relinquished?

It is not clear what is within and what is without, what is
landscape and what is the soul's terrain. All is still,
convictionless, expectant.

Where is this inner place where nothing is clear?

Is it the centre of the exploding heart of God, silence just a
pause before love breaks its barrier?

Or is this abandonment?

I walk.

Let's take stock of where we have got to so far in our exploration
of faith identity. We began with an account of the spiritual pain
and hurt that can arise for one who doubts, and tried to uncover
what such doubt might mean. Through that process, we un-
covered some dominant assumptions at work in popular notions
of what constitutes faith identity: the centrality of a given corpus
of teaching; the need for individual assent to and agreement with
that teaching; and the expectation that certain forms of religious
expression will flow from it as a proof of commitment. We called
this a 'vicious triangle' of doctrine, belief and expression, and
tried to prise this apart, looking at its constituent parts, and the
relationship between them. As with other aspects of human
identity, we discovered that power differentials between human
beings are important here: those with power define the bound-

aries of acceptability for doctrine and belief, which are then portrayed as neutral and universal, when in fact they are partial and contestable. This explains why those on the underside of power, down the ages, have again and again challenged the content of faith traditions, usually at great personal cost. It also explains why faith traditions and belief-systems change all the time. Albeit slowly. It is of their nature, because they are human.

I say all this not to rubbish faith institutions, or to claim that they are redundant or without worth. In the case of Christianity, two thousand years of human creativity and imagination engaging with the divine gives us a rich, varied and diverse corpus of resources on which to draw in our contemporary search for ultimate meaning and value. Dialogue between God and human beings down the ages is crucial to the enrichment of the continuation of that conversation today. I am suggesting, however, that we need more critical awareness about how power works in defining the boundaries of faith – in deciding who are outsiders and who are insiders; who should be listened to and who can be dismissed. We need more agnosticism about where Truth lies, since none of us knows the final answer to that question. We need less deference, and fewer assumptions that religious leaders and theologians have any privileged access to the Truth. And we need to feel more empowered to discover for ourselves the truths that lie at the heart of our lives and the depth of our souls. We need to know that just because a human institution takes as its focus an awareness of the divine, this does not make that institution itself divine.

Faith honours uniqueness

This book opened with an encounter with a child called Glyn, and a discussion of the miracle of his absolute uniqueness across time and space. Our conclusion was that there is no one else in this universe that is quite like him, and there never will be again, and that the same is true for all of us. We also concluded that our uniqueness is intended. It is a divine gift. We are meant to revel in it, to love ourselves, and appreciate our glorious one-offness. Subsequently, we explored the choice that faces each of us as we encounter others: the choice between opening up and closing down, and said that our response will relate closely to our personal history of empowerment and disempowerment – a story that is also unique to us.

The danger with doctrine, as explored earlier in this chapter, is that it disregards the miracle of human uniqueness. It demands the same from everybody, and does not pay enough attention to our stories and their specificity. Faith communities that are built on such doctrines can become places where we assume commonality with one another, and begin to tell one another what we must think and feel, rather than asking one another who we think we are, and who God is to us. This habit of telling rather than asking is endemic within the Christian community. It is particularly acute around issues of faith and belief (our love for God), and issues of sexuality and relationships (our love for one another). Though not explicitly designed to critique this aspect of institutional Christian life, Carl Rogers' person-centred philosophy offers an apposite and accurate summary of what is at stake. In his terminology, we *fail to honour our subjective experience*. Here's a quote from his book *A Way of Being* that expresses powerfully what can happen when a person's uniqueness is honoured by another:

I find, both in therapeutic interviews and in the intensive group experiences which have meant a great deal to me, that hearing has consequences. When I truly hear a person and the meanings that are important to him at any moment, hearing not simply his words, but him, and when I let him know that I have heard his own private personal meanings, many things happen. There is first of all a grateful look. He feels released. He wants to tell me more about his world. He surges forth in a new sense of freedom. He becomes more open to the process of change.

I have noticed that the more deeply I hear the meaning of

this person, the more there is that happens. Almost always, when the person realizes he has been deeply heard, his eyes moisten. I think in some real sense he is weeping for joy. It is as though he were saying, 'Thank God, somebody has heard me. Someone knows what it's like to be me.' . . . By that one simple response he is released from his loneliness; he has become a human being again. There are many, many people living in private dungeons today, people who give no evidence of it whatsoever on the outside, where you have to listen very sharply to hear the faint messages from the dungeon.[3]

Elsewhere in the same book he says:

One of the most satisfying feelings I know – and also one of the most growth-promoting experiences for the other person – comes from my appreciating this individual in the same way that I appreciate a sunset. People are just as wonderful as sunsets if I can let them *be*. In fact, perhaps the reason we can truly appreciate a sunset is that we cannot control it. When I look at a sunset as I did the other evening, I don't find myself saying, 'soften the orange a little on the right hand corner, and put a bit more purple along the base, and use a little more pink in the cloud color.' I don't do that. I don't *try* to control a sunset. I watch it with awe as it unfolds. I like myself best when I can appreciate my staff member, my son, my daughter, my grandchildren, in this same way. I believe this is a somewhat Oriental attitude; for me it is a most satisfying one.[4]

If we believe in the mysterious and miraculous uniqueness of each and every human being on this earth, and that this originates in God, the Generator Of Diversity, then faith communities should be, first and foremost, places of unconditional acceptance; places of liberation from loneliness. Interestingly, it was Rogers' perception that institutionalized religion fails, almost by definition, to honour subjective experience and human uniqueness, that led him away from a vocation to ordination and into a lifetime as a therapist. Drawing on Rogers' insights, it is clear that we need models of faith identity that involve a lot less locking in dungeons, and a lot more appreciation of the miracle of human sunsets. Until, as a Christian community, we can listen to people's experience, honour it, and come to terms with the diversity of lived reality, we stand in the way of human growth and change. And insofar as we hinder people's growth, we cannot expect people's allegiance.

Faith is communal

Hand in hand with a celebration of our uniqueness comes the recognition of our limitation, and our acute need for one another. At the beginning of this book this led us to critique our contemporary society's over-valuing of individual autonomy. And in rethinking notions of faith identity, we must revisit this insight.

Each of us is a tiny, albeit indispensable, part of the whole. The same is true of faith traditions. Christianity, for instance, in its many different forms, is just a part of a much wider and broader canvas that is humanity's engagement with God throughout the ages and across the world. To the extent that we claim the Christian tradition as our own, we recognize our need for it, and we value its insights (while also being alert to the power dynamics at work within it). But we also need to be aware of its limitations. It is desirable for us to live in a constant and active dialogue with it – learning about it, exploring it, running at times from it, turning back to it and making it, as far as possible, a focus for dynamic spiritual explorations.

This may feel like an individual journey. Indeed, it may sometimes feel like a very lonely one. But faith journeys are never individual. They cannot be. Faith is communal because our souls are communal. I do not mean by this that faith is about groups of people with shared belief-systems engaging in corporate activities (though religion is often precisely that). I mean that faith always takes me out of myself. It involves stretching beyond myself to something that transcends the limits of 'me' (though is deeply connected to what is within me). Whether we are aware of it or not, we are shaped and formed by the faith stories of others, across generations as well as in the here and now. The human spiritual imagination is alive and at work all over the world, all of the time. What we do with our embodied souls as groups of human beings creates truth in ways that individuals cannot know. The making sacred of spaces and places; the symbolization of people and things; the ritualization of everyday activities: through all these things we access our primal spiritual heritage in ways that we will never fully understand or consciously know. Yet we may feel the power; we may be emotionally moved; we may sense the presence of mystery. But none of these things happens because we are alone, even if we think we are alone when they happen to us. Gazing upon Stonehenge or Glastonbury Tor; watching bathers in the Ganges or rows of Muslim men at prayer; staring into a flickering candle flame or listening to the crashing of waves on a beach; feeling awe-struck at the birth of a new life, or grief stricken at a life's end; moving in circles or dancing in firelight; catching our breath over the impossible accuracy of a poetic image, or crying with the expression of yearning through melody; eating bread and drinking wine to remember a particular person and a particular story. Through all these things we are sharing in the expression of connections to the earth, to other human beings, and to the unarguable forces of nature to which, in the end, we are all subject. There is no reason why we should not be open to all of this: embrace it all, learn from it, feel the connection with our primal heritage – our common soul.

Faith is made

The famous eighteenth-century preacher and Anglican, John Wesley, the founder of Methodism, was both powerful and charismatic. Yet before his heart was famously 'strangely warmed' (i.e. prior to the moment he considered to be his conversion) he worried about his faith. He wrote to a friend of his, a Moravian by the name of Peter Böhler, and voiced his concern that until he could banish his feelings of ambivalence, he was not fit to preach. Böhler's response was unequivocal. He counselled Wesley that in no way should he give up. Instead he advised, 'Preach faith 'til you have it.'

Post-modern philosophers would say that Böhler's remedy deployed the notion of 'performativity'. This concept reverses the usual order of things. In our popular conception of faith identity as explored at the beginning of this chapter, we saw how belief (in the form of intellectual assent) was assumed to come first, followed by the expression of that belief. Performativity says that the opposite can be the case. Belief can be generated from activity. In other words you can express faith, for example by taking part in rituals, from a position of not believing or not knowing, and this can have a profound faith-generating effect. Behaving as though something were the case can help to shape within us a sense that it actually is the case. That is, faith and belief can be created through religious expression, they do not have to exist as a prerequisite.

The precise relationship between believing and belonging has been in question for some time. It has become clear that, in relation to organized religion, not only can people believe and not belong (that is, retain their faith in God but leave the Church), they can also belong without believing. Those who perceive themselves both to believe *and* belong have often found manifestations of the latter problematic. Heterosexual couples who wish to express their residual sense of belonging to the Christian community by getting married in church, even though they are no longer regular worshippers, are frowned upon; parents who want their children to have a sense of belonging to a faith community through infant baptism are suspected of 'cheating' – gaining benefits for their children without demonstrating the requisite commitment themselves. But a model of faith that has escaped the vicious triangle of doctrine, belief and expression will be relaxed about believing and belonging, aware that the relationship between them is complex and unpredictable, and that expressing what we perceive only dimly can transform us in unexpected ways.

For years I worried that I had no spiritual practice and that my faith identity was therefore lost. Church was impossible; the alternatives I explored were worse. But while I avoided both church and its alternatives, I was engaged in deep and challenging friendships and love relationships; I was stretched into deep questioning about justice and integrity in my writing and in my work; and I was often moved deeply when in silent dialogue with natural phenomena – especially the sea. And one day it became clear to me, with a sudden sense of liberation, that all of those latter things were themselves my spiritual practice, whether or not I coupled them with more conventional expressions of faith. The identity crisis I felt in the teeth of the vicious triangle gave way to a realization that I had been focusing on the wrong things. Other questions emerged as more important: what makes me feel alive? When do I feel expanded, enhanced and challenged? When do I feel most strongly and intimately connected with others? In short, what opportunities is God offering for divine encounter, and how can I respond?

Encountering God

Can the sea be God to me?
You speak to me of yearning,
tendril-fingers laced together
making love waves spread,
rhythmic, slow.
Paradox of summer day,
iced surface reflecting sky
breaking into earth tones

near the shoreline.
Swell of change, moving from beneath,
brings foaming eruption,
fleeing dissipation.

Can the sky be God to me?
Lying beneath you,
open face, open body
feeling the weight of your lightness
holding me in place
I stare into you.
You reach down,
touchless, voiceless, expansive connection.
Your cloud canvas is ever-changing,
countless imperceptible shifts
draw beauty from movement,
edging slowly away.

Can the earth be God to me?
Hard splintering, warm crumbling
dry sand runs through my fingers,
heavy injuring stones hurt
when I'm digging for surety.
Giving, withholding
excess, deprivation.
This is how I know you.

Can you be God to me?
What more could I desire
beyond your depth of understanding?
I am already undone.
Where else would I go if you disappeared?
What other meaning would I derive
that you could not show me?
Mystery and love are one.

What is it about God that we do not understand?

If God is the originator of our mysterious uniqueness, then we can assume that God, and only God, knows fully who we are. God, and only God, knows the particular combination of empowerment and disempowerment that has formed us – in particular, that has formed our faith identity. Therefore only God knows what kind of encounter with God will enable us to open up, rather than close down, and therefore what spiritual expression and activity is appropriate for us at any given moment in our personal history. I become a lover of God by being open to God in ways that God shows me.

Earlier in this book we explored, in some depth, the dynamics of how our identity is formed through intimacy with others. We discovered that the challenge in interpersonal encounter is to find ways to 'start our thinking with the other, not with the self. We need not to include but to distance, not to grasp but to let loose. The challenge is to let them disclose themselves.' Peter Schmid's insight has, perhaps, an even more acute relevance in the context of encountering God.

It is easy to see how we make God like ourselves in order to understand God. Much of our theology does precisely that, and the discipline itself well understands this irony at its own heart. The Christian tradition has always held two perceived characteristics of God in tension: that God is 'wholly other' (and therefore mysterious and unknowable), and that God is within us, closer to us than our own souls and therefore deeply knowable. If theology intellectualizes and systematizes all that human beings can justifiably and reliably say about God, then perhaps mysticism restores the balance and offers a necessary corrective. In exploring encounters with other people we discovered that the 'felt self' was the locus of reliability – to repeat the insight of theologian Sebastian Moore, 'You are what you feel. It is in feeling happy, or angry, or sad, or hopeful, in response to an event, that I touch base with myself. My *identity* lights up in one of these *feelings*.'[5] It is the mystical tradition that highlights the possibility of connecting with God at the level of feeling; of becoming convinced of God's unconditional and infinite love through a process that does not foreground the intellect. The underlying perception at the heart of mysticism is that God both passionately loves human beings, and also – amazingly – likes them. The unconditional love and acceptance that Rogers suggests that one human being can begin to have for another is perfected in the love that God has for each unique human being, because the divine has a perfect understanding of the texture and nuances of our souls.

'Believing in' God's love for us in a mystical sense is very different from the kind of 'believing in' that we do when we make something into a doctrine. For as soon as we do that, we make God's love something that we can fail to believe in, or cease to believe in, and then it becomes part of the problem. 'I am absolutely beloved of God' isn't an equivalent statement to 'Jesus died, was buried, descended into hell and on the third day he rose again'. It is not, in short, something that we can assent to intellectually, or fail to assent to. It is a felt reality that we can simply aim to become increasingly aware of through the spiritual practice that such love encourages within us.

Taking our cue from what we learned about encountering others, we might suggest that the aim of our spiritual practice is to develop skills of intimacy with God. The prioritization of feeling over thinking; of asking over telling; and the role of courage, emotional imagination and humility, all have a resonance in this context. What does it mean to be 'face to face' with God? Where are the overlapping hinterlands where we have a sense of knowing God, and where are the places of non-overlap, the places of challenge? How do we live the dialogue between the ways in which we know God and the ways in which God is strange to us, or cannot be known – or can be known in one way one day, and not known in that way the next?

We need courage to 'ask God', but only because there is a weight of tradition about what is allowed and what is disqualified in our questioning of God. All are spun from theological systems that may be irrelevant to us in our uniqueness. If we construe the process of asking as being a feeling process more than a thinking one, then the possibility emerges of non-specific asking. That is, we can relate to God not so much through the asking of particular questions, but simply by being open to God, by being a question, by living in the humility and openness of not knowing.

Being faithful

My final suggestion, then, is that 'being faithful' is not about inhabiting the vicious triangle in the right way. It is about a courageous opening of the heart to the otherness of the divine – an otherness that will never be understood, only felt, and then only a tiny bit at a time.

In our consideration of what it means to encounter another person, we concluded that 'Really knowing somebody comes from a sense of a growing familiarity with their emotional landscape. What is it that brings tears of sadness to their eyes? When are they delighted, and what makes them respond with joy?' We suggested that it is emotional imagination that enables us to begin to know these things about another. So my final question is this: how can we bring our emotional imagination to a heart-to-heart encounter with God?

One place to start is with the flesh and blood person who shows us who God is. What follows, therefore, is a meditation on the person of Jesus as portrayed in the four Gospels. My aim is not to set out a systematic account of Jesus' identity, or to make suggestions as to how we should all understand him. It is simply my partial, subjective, imaginative encounter with the Jesus that I find in the Gospels, and expresses something of my current understanding of what it means to be faithful.

Who do you say that I am?

You are your heritage
Your story doesn't make sense unless we go back 42 generations. There were 14 generations from Abraham to David, another 14

from David to the deportation to Babylon, another 14 from the deportation to the Messiah. You are named Messiah from the very beginning, and so put in your place. But the meaning of that place is what matters and this must unfold. It cannot be given whole. You have to make it.

This multitude of generations is the depth of your roots. The spread of this vast, intricate web of connections is the capacious space within which you find yourself. Your 'home' is a bloodline, an inheritance and a weight of expectation. This is your raw material.

The strange circumstances of your conception alert your kin to the certainty that you will be different, special. And so it begins before you are even born: the investment in who you will become, the dreaming about what you will achieve for your people, the imagining of you.

When you are born, an angel tells the shepherds that you are a Saviour, the Messiah, the Lord. Simeon recognizes you as God's salvation, and speaks of your destiny in a way that underlines that it cannot yet be fully grasped, merely hinted at. You are to be the cause of the falling and the rising of many, you will be a sign that will be opposed. The inner thoughts of many will be revealed because of you. He says, too, that a sword will pierce your mother's soul. With joy uppermost, she cannot hear this.

Back in Galilee you grow and become strong. You are clever too, filled with wisdom. At 12 you accompany your parents to Jerusalem for the festival of the Passover, staying behind afterwards, not telling them. Your parents have to search for three days before they find you in the Temple, among the teachers, listening to them and asking questions. You call the Temple your father's house. You are at home there.

Now you are an adult, ready to strike out on your own, to create and to discover your destiny. You are recognized and baptized by your kinsman, John, who defers to you as the greater. Where he baptizes with water, he says, you will baptize with the Holy Spirit and with fire. The voice of God comes to you, affirming your belovedness and your sonship. You embrace it all.

You set out as an itinerant, a traveller. Wherever you go, you make your mark. The strong roots of your heritage have made you a person of stature. You cannot be ignored, you never go unnoticed. You are attractive and charismatic, you are grounded and impressive. The authority with which you speak comes from the breadth of your connections and the depth of your tradition. You speak from experience that is beyond yourself alone. You manifest a deep personal power. You quickly become famous for your rhetoric and your miraculous works. The word spreads.

One day you try to go back. Back to your home town, where you were brought up. In the synagogue they hand you the Scriptures and you get up to speak. They see how impressive you have become. At first they are proud, but soon they are unnerved. You try to explain to them that the Scriptures they know so well – that part of Isaiah that promises freedom and liberation – have been fulfilled. You are bringing them good news. You are the anointed one. But they turn on you. They are enraged. Why? Because you are transgressing their expectations of you. They know who you are. Who on earth do you think you are, saying such grandiose things? They are convinced of the rightful limits of what 'one of them' can hope for and achieve. You are daring to surpass these limits. You hold up the possibility of greatness and they cannot imagine it from within their own people. So they cast you out and reject you. They feel safer with you gone.

You are deeply affected by this rejection, and by their unbelief. You cannot perform deeds of power in that place. Is this when you decide that home, family and kin must mean more than the obvious? You begin to extend the definitions, to expand your household. You adopt those who are not your kin to be your kin, and encourage others to do likewise. When your mother and brothers seek you out, you ask, 'Who are my mother and my brothers?' Not because you want to disown, reject or belittle your bloodline or your family, but because you want, simply, to extend the reaches of your heritage. You say that whoever does the will of God is a member of your family. Indeed, when the woman who has been bleeding for 12 years touches your cloak and is healed, you call her 'daughter' because of her faith. From the cross you hand over the care of your mother to your closest friend, saying, 'Woman, here is your son'; you say to him, 'Here is your mother.'

Your genealogy gives you a place to begin. The prophets of your people guide your path and give structure and meaning to your life – they feed and inform your sense of purpose. Your heritage gives you the tools for understanding yourself: where you fit in the scheme of things. It is your touchstone and you go back to it at every significant moment of your life. It is also how you explain to others who you are and what your life is for. On the road to Emmaus, for instance, when it is all over, you explain to the disciples how everything that has happened can be understood through a certain reading of the Scriptures.

Yet you do not inhabit this tradition and heritage in a way that restricts you. It opens up your identity and provides a myriad possibilities for you. Yours is not a life lived between narrow, predetermined lines, for it is your love of God, and your love of those whom God sends to you that drives your work, and that enables you to carry on.

You are your heritage, but you are much more than your heritage alone.

You are what you do and say

At first, what you do is all that people have to go on as they puzzle over who you are. You heal a sick man at the Sheep Gate in Jerusalem. He has waited 38 years for a chance to get near to the waters that he believes will cure him. But you invite him to pick up his mat and walk. To him you are simply 'the man who made me well'. Others want to know, 'Who is the man who made you well?' He has no answer beyond what he knows by experience.

You meet a Samaritan woman by a well and have a long conversation. She is astonished that you know so much about her that you have no reason to know. She recognizes you as a prophet, as someone with a powerful gift that can transform her life. She wants her friends and family to know you too, and says to them, 'Come and see the man who told me everything I have ever done.'

Again, you are 'the man who . . .'

And after you calm the storm that threatens the lives of your disciples, they ask, in awe, 'Who then is this, that even the winds and the sea obey him?'

You encourage this piecing together of your identity from the evidence. When the disciples of John are sent to you for confirmation that you are 'he who is to come', you answer like this: 'Go and tell John what you have seen and heard: the blind receive their sight, the lame walk, the lepers are cleansed, the deaf hear, the dead are raised, the poor have good news brought to them. And blessed is anyone who takes no offence at me.'

In other words, in the transformation of others, we see and know you.

Everything you do is about unleashing the power within, liberating gifts within people that only you can see. You are about setting people free, cutting them loose. Those thus freed give themselves to you. They want to commit; they desire to follow. Those with an investment in un-freedom feel differently. They are at home with the way things are – a world with winners and losers, where they are, or hope to be, the winners. They feel threatened by your actions and by your message. Freedom for others means, they think, disruption and loss for themselves. You know this, and you are angered by their hardness of heart, especially as they are supposed to be the spiritual leaders of your people.

On the Sabbath they lie in wait for you to trap you into breaking the law. There is a man with a withered hand. What will you do? Will you heal him? Of course you do – without shame or regret. You are clear: it is better to do good than harm; better to do good than to do nothing, even if you break religious rules in the process. When an opportunity to respond to need presents itself, you take it – there and then. You do not wait for another day. You pluck ears of corn because you and your disciples are hungry now. You heal those who need it today. You speak to the leaders of your people with deep challenge and offer them a sharp critique. Why not offer liberation on the Sabbath, of all days, rather than seeing healing as 'work' that must be forbidden? You point out that, according to their own rules, animals can be saved from drowning, but human beings cannot be healed of their infirmities. Where is the sense in this?

And when it's not the Sabbath you offend by mixing with the wrong kinds of people. Tax collectors and sinners are coming near to listen to you. The Pharisees and the scribes are grumbling and saying, 'This fellow welcomes sinners and eats with them.'

Who is the man who behaves in this way?

He is the one who preaches about the kingdom of God, where the first shall be last, and the last first. People will come from east and west and be accepted, you say, but those who think they have a right to it will be thrown out. The humble will be exalted, the exalted, humbled. You say to the Pharisees, 'You are those who justify yourselves in the sight of others, but God knows your hearts, for what is prized by human beings is an abomination in the sight of God.' You tell them parables to reinforce your point: the lost sheep; the lost coin. You talk of rejoicing in heaven, and of joy over the sinner who repents. You revel in disproportionality and exaggeration. Leave one hundred and pursue only one. That is your logic – the logic of preciousness and excess, of joy and love. Your climax is the story of the prodigal son, for every hearer has to choose: whose side am I on? With whom do I identify? Whose perspective do I share? Can I rejoice in the gratuitous love that the son is given, or am I resentful of it for its unfairness? You show us the kingdom of God when you set people free, and you show it in your stories about what freedom looks like.

You present us with a clear question: what kind of world do we really want? A world where everyone gets what they deserve? Or a world where there is outrageous, undeserved generosity, where people receive what only God knows they need? Your actions and your choices manifest the latter. Your teaching reinforces this. Layer upon layer, doing and saying, saying and doing, you show us who you are, and you spell out your message in a way that children find easy and adults find difficult. In a way that the downtrodden welcome with tears of relief, and the powerful resent with tears of rage – tears that fuel, before long, a murderous intent.

What you do and say will be the death of you.

You are passionate

You are deeply emotional. You are a complex and constantly changing character, given to extremes. There is an immediacy and an urgency about you, a capacity to be deeply affected and to show it. This is what attracts people to you and makes you a leader. You are famous – a celebrity, mobbed by the crowds wherever you go.

You are a provocative teacher, full of exaggeration, rhetoric and humour. Your sayings are over the top: you speak of the cutting off of sinning hands, the tearing out of eyes. Your images are arresting: of asking for bread and being given a stone, asking for fish and being given a snake. You warn of wolves in sheep's clothing. Your examples reveal a keen, observant mind – one that has spotted what happens to old wineskins when new wine is put in them; that has learned what happens to rulers with grand ideas but no strategy. You paint verbal pictures of those whose wealth has blunted their sensibility, those whose greed drives them to barbarity. And you notice the small, apparently unimportant people, those that others overlook. You know that they are open to your message of transformation, and that once transformed they will move mountains for love of you.

People are astounded by your teaching and your sense of authority. Yet you too are capable of being amazed by others. The Roman centurion, for instance – too humble to have you under his roof – recognizes in you a kindred spirit; one with awesome power. His faith in you is unwavering, stemming from the surety of his own position, which in turn is granted by someone more powerful still. You say that no one in Israel has demonstrated faith like this. Then you are taken aback by the insistence of another non-Jew, a Canaanite woman whom you ignore, who shouts at you persistently, wanting you to heal her demon-possessed daughter. You say, 'I was sent only to the lost sheep of the house of Israel . . . It is not fair to take the children's food and throw it to the dogs.' To which she replies, 'Yes, Lord, yet even the dogs eat the crumbs that fall from the master's table.' She makes you see things differently. Again, you declare, 'Great is your faith! Let it be done for you as you wish.'

There is no middle way with you. People either follow you, offering their total commitment, or they run away and beg you to leave them alone. In the end, many hate you. The whole town of the Gerasenes responds to you as one. They fear your power, for you cure Legion – the rejected one who lives as a wild animal among tombstones, possessed by many demons. Somehow they prefer the status quo – where Legion's superhuman strength could at any time be turned against them – to the sight of him sitting at your feet, clothed and in his right mind. The change is too big to take. They cannot be near this kind of liberating power. They ask that you leave them be – go back to where you came from.

Sometimes you want to be left alone, but it's rarely possible for long. The crowds always seek you out. Despite your need for solitude, your response to them is always one of compassion. You see their need; their hunger for your teaching. When you hear about the beheading of John, you withdraw in a boat to a deserted place by yourself. But the crowds follow you on foot. You are grieving for your kinsman – a traumatic and horrific death for the one whose fate has been so closely intertwined with your own, even from before your birth; the one who set you going in your mission, affirming your perception of your role, confirming your vocation. Yet in spite of your loss of all of that, when you go ashore you see a great crowd waiting expectantly for you and you respond. You cure their sick. You think they are like sheep without a shepherd. You give of yourself beyond enduring. You spend yourself, just like you say others should. I guess you know there isn't much time.

You desire others around you, especially the 12 you choose to be your friends. They are special to you, and you give them responsibilities. You explain everything to them. They are the ones to whom you do not speak in parables. You give it to them straight. You look after them, too. When they return from being sent out to preach and to heal in your name, they want to tell you everything, and you take them away so you can be by yourselves in a lonely place to rest. You trust them with your story and attempt to include them in what's going to happen to you. They don't understand at first, but you keep trying to help them to see it. You trust, you include, you explain. Again and again. In the end, they get in the way. Their love for you leads them to want to protect you from a fate they cannot believe must befall you, given who you are. They just don't get it. You know that they can't, and they won't, but you love them anyway. You say, 'I have called you friends.' How well you know them, these friends. You understand that Judas will betray you, and why he finds that necessary. You know that Peter will deny you and bitterly regret it. And you know that your friends will scatter after your death. Perhaps you also know that the women will remain with you, watch with you, through the mysterious time between your death and rising again. You know that Mary will be there, the first to greet you.

For others you reserve your anger and your sharp wit. In the run-up to death your feelings are closer to the surface. You are given to histrionics (cursing the fig tree for its lack of fruit, though it is out of season), you make grand gestures (marching into the city on a donkey causing a commotion). You are also moved to compassion (you restore the sight of two blind men when they request it, and they immediately follow you), and anger (in the Temple, turning tables and wielding a stick). You withdraw to Bethany. You give everything you have in your last few days. You face the constant traps from the Pharisees, Scribes and Sadducees, but you outwit them all. They want you arrested, but they fear the crowds. You make the most of this, unleashing the full force of your passionate critique, without holding back.

You call them whitewashed tombs, full of the bones of the dead; they are snakes, a brood of vipers. You say they clean the outside of the cup and dish, while leaving the inside full of greed and wickedness. You ask them, how do they think they can escape being sentenced to hell?

The joke is that that's precisely what they thought they had in store for you.

You are mysterious

Wherever you go, the demons know exactly who you are. Your very presence torments them. Legion's demons ask you, 'What have you to do with us, Jesus, Son of the Most High God?' It's a good question. What, indeed, is the commonality between you and a bunch of unclean spirits? Your response reveals that nothing and no one is beyond relationship with you and, by extension, with God. You negotiate with them. They beg you to allow them to find homes in a herd of swine, rather than simply be cast out with nowhere to go. You accede to their request.

But again and again you silence demons lest they get in the way of others understanding who you are. You want people to discover your identity for themselves, to encounter you and experience you. You want people to taste you, to hear your words, to be puzzled and confused; to work hard for an understanding of the riddle of you. You forbid shortcuts in that process. So you generate an impossibly rich and varied array of images and metaphors, each highlighting a different aspect of your self. You are the light of the world, the bread of life, the gate of the sheep, the good shepherd, the true vine, the resurrection and the life. You are Teacher and Lord, the way, the truth and the life. You are always oblique. You never disclose yourself in a way that would divert your hearers from their own explorations. You put forward a plural self-understanding, and a constantly changing one. You also like people to discover you through dialogue: 'Who do others say I am?', 'And you, who do you say that I am?' Your identity is relational.

And from those who make accurate declarations about you, more is demanded. You require from them a fuller appreciation of the meanings and the implications of any statement of your identity. This is how it happens on the mountain top. Peter, James and John are with you. You know that they see you conversing with Moses and Elijah. They hear a voice from heaven saying, 'This is my son, the beloved, with him I am well pleased. Listen to him.' Could your identity be any clearer? And finally, they see you transfigured. They feel the power of God and they are deeply afraid. But you know that they have little grasp of the meaning of it all. You explain that you will be betrayed into human hands, be made to suffer, be killed and rise again, but they do not want to hear this. The rebuke of Peter who would prevent it leads to you exclaiming, 'Get behind me, Satan! You are a stumbling block to me; for you are setting your mind not on divine things but on human things.'

You want people's appreciation of you to go far beyond the intellect alone. You warm to those who grasp who you are at deeper levels than just the mind. The woman who anoints you with perfume for burial, wiping your feet with her hair, has a visceral intuition of your importance, and the significance of what is about to happen to you. She expresses this with her body. You accord her deep respect and declare that throughout the ages, she will be remembered. Similarly with the thief on the cross who connects instinctively with your goodness and the fact that you have done nothing to deserve this cruel death. He asks that you remember him in your kingdom, and you respond to his deep and immediate grasp of reality, promising him a place beside you in paradise.

At the Last Supper, you do a beautiful thing. You make promises with yourself. You give your friends your own body and blood in the symbolic form of bread and wine. You say that 'Whoever eats me will live because of me.' So you show your friends that we are to do more than simply recognize who you are; we are to incorporate you into who we are – to take you in, to fuse with you, to become one with you. To be changed by you.

And again, on the road to Emmaus, after hours of discussion and intellectual debate about the prophets and the Scriptures, your friends finally recognize you when you break the bread at dinner. And immediately you vanish from their sight. Once you have gone they remember how they felt when you were speaking to them about the Scriptures: 'Were not our hearts burning within us?' they said.

You filled them with energy and passion. They burned for you, but did not know it.

At the end, you are silent

On the Mount of Olives you are praying alone. The disciples are a stone's throw away. There, but not there. You pray, in anguish, for the cup to be removed. Is it worse that you know so much, or better? You have studied the Scripture. You understand the prophecies. You know your genealogy, your heritage, your story, your history. So you know your destiny too.

And you know how power works. That people want it for themselves. You understand identity structured by self-importance. You know that you have exposed this among the powerful. You know what you have undermined, challenged, subverted. You wanted no power for yourself, and this is what they could not understand. You need no power because you know exactly who you are. You have nothing to prove by undermining others. Nothing to prove by putting your case. Your case has been put: through compassionate action and insightful teaching. You have given without counting the cost; given disproportionately, unfairly, because you perceived need to be disproportionate, unfair. You have gone out in vulnerability (with nothing, dependent). You have received from all those who would give: self-satisfied Pharisees out to trick you; women with nothing to give but perfume and tears; tax collectors curious about a better and more just way of living – changed by just one dinner with you.

You have been a process held open – an emerging identity. Tighter definition would have violated others' choice to recognize you for who you are to them.

So you asked, you did not tell:

Who do the crowds say that I am?

And you, who do you say that I am?

Now you stand before the Elders, the people, and before Pilate. They want to know: are you the Messiah? The Son of God? The King of the Jews?

You say that I am.

You say so.

If you say so.

You know that even if they speak the truth, if they do not believe it, then it cannot be the truth for them. So you will not play their game. You choose, instead, to listen to the silence of your heart.

You are silent. It is a dignified silence; a refusal to retaliate or to correct. It is a refusal to take control of what they make of you. In silence you remain resolutely yourself.

So we are back in Gethsemane, where your sweat is like drops of blood, because the strength you seek is the strength we all need: the strength to be yourself. To embrace all that that means. To go through with it, in its entirety. To see it through to its logical conclusion. For, as you put it: what does it profit us to gain the whole world, but to lose or to forfeit ourselves?

5

Extending ourselves

———•———

Open/ing

The world bleeds through,
outside finds a way
inside, through
the gaps I knew and
surprise fissures
I didn't know
how deep.

Caught breath, arrested beat,
compression
follows dilation,
my heart floods
runs over, outraged
at its smallness
for this birthing.

Shaken, indignant,
the mind
reinscribes protection,
shy transmutations move
inwards, waiting until
I can bear again
the world's bleeding.

The nature of gift

For this final stage in our consideration of human identity I would like to take as my focus a wonderful book by Lewis Hyde, entitled *The Gift: How the Creative Spirit Transforms the World*. It is a work that is inspirational on many counts, but is particularly helpful in discovering new models of identity that enable us to embrace change, negotiate power, and honour both our own uniqueness and that of others. In the first half of the book, Hyde lays out a theory of gift in an engaging and multi-disciplinary way, drawing on folk wisdom and stories, anthropology, sociology, and on psychological and spiritual insights. In the second half he applies this theory to the life of the artist – in part as a way of working out his own identity as a poet. Both aspects of the book are richly applicable to a consideration of who we are as spiritual beings, and what it is we are called to in 'being ourselves'. Before we can explore these parallels, it is first of all necessary to give a brief account of Hyde's thinking.

His opening assumption is

> that a work of art is a gift, not a commodity. Or, to state the modern case with more precision, that works of art exist simultaneously in two 'economies', a market economy and a gift economy. Only one of these is essential, however. A work of art can survive without the market, but where there is no gift there is no art.[1]

He continues by making it clear that a gift does not come to us through our own efforts. 'We cannot buy it; we cannot acquire it through an act of will. It is bestowed upon us.'[2] As an artist works, some proportion of the work is perceived to be 'bestowed' upon him or her. As Hyde puts it, 'the artist does not find himself engaged or exhilarated by the work, nor does it seem authentic, until this gratuitous element has appeared, so that along with any true creation comes the uncanny sense that "I", the artist, did not make the work'.[3] Hyde then extends these two senses of gift to the work after it has left the hands of the artist:

> art that matters to us – which moves the heart, or revives the soul, or delights the senses, or offers courage for living, however we choose to describe the experience – that work is received by us as a gift is received. Even if we have paid a fee at the door of the museum or concert hall, when we are touched by a work of art something comes to us which has nothing to do with the price . . . We may not have the power to profess our gifts as the artist does, and yet we come to recognize, and in a sense to receive, the endowments of our being through the agency of his creation. We feel fortunate, even redeemed . . . When we are moved by art we are grateful that the artist lived, grateful that he labored in the service of his gifts.[4]

Hyde's exploration of the theory of gift is complex and multifaceted, but for our purposes there are four key insights:

1 The gift must always move

Whatever is given must always be passed on, not kept. Or, if it is kept, then something of similar value must move on in its stead. 'You may keep your Christmas present, but it ceases to be a gift in the true sense unless you have given something else away. As it is passed along, the gift may be given back to the original donor, but this is not essential.'[5] In folk tales, the person who tries to hold on to a gift often dies. According to Hyde, tribal peoples usually distinguish between gifts and capital, and one man's gift may not become another man's capital. If it does, something horrible happens. So if a man receives a goat as a gift, he might throw a big party at which everybody gets fed (so passing on the gift). But he may not set the goat aside to produce milk and more goats.[6]

Another way of describing the motion of the gift is, Hyde suggests,

> to say that a gift must always be used up, consumed, eaten. *The gift is property that perishes* . . . Food is one of the most common images for the gift because it is so obviously consumed. Even when a gift is not food, when it is something we would think of as a durable good, it is often referred to as a thing to be eaten. Shell necklaces and armbands are the ritual gifts in the Trobriand Islands and when they are passed from one group to the next, protocol demands that the man who gives them away toss them on the ground and say, 'Here, some food we could not eat.'[7]

2 Gifts are erotic

While the sale of a commodity leaves no necessary connection between people, a gift establishes a bond of fellow-feeling. Hyde calls this an 'erotic bond', and suggests that while a gift economy is characterized by '*eros*', the economy of trade is characterized by '*logos*'. That is, by neutrality and fixed boundaries. Gifts are agents of social cohesion, while trade keeps spheres independent. Gift-giving creates momentum, whereas trade maintains stasis – payment keeping things in balance. Hyde sums up:

> We might best picture the difference between gifts and commodities in this regard by imagining two territories separated by a boundary. A gift, when it moves across the boundary, either stops being a gift or else abolishes the boundary. A commodity can cross the line without any change in its nature; moreover, its exchange will often establish a boundary where none previously existed (as, for example, in the sale of a necessity to a friend). *Logos*-trade draws the boundary, *eros*-trade erases it.[8]

3 Gifts grow as they are given away

There is a paradox at the heart of gift exchange – that is, when a gift is used, it is not used up. The opposite is in fact the case. If a gift is not used, it will be lost, while the gift that is passed on remains abundant. As Hyde says:

> In the world of gift . . . you not only can have your cake and eat it too, you can't have your cake *unless* you eat it. Gift exchange and erotic life are connected in this regard. The gift is an emanation of Eros, and therefore to speak of gifts that survive their use is to describe a natural fact: libido is not lost when it is given away. Eros never wastes his lovers.[9]

4 Gifts gravitate to those who need them most

Hyde shows us how gifts tend to move in circles, and that the gift moves in the direction of the empty place – that is, towards the one who has been without the longest. But if someone appears elsewhere whose need is greater, the gift leaves its familiar channel, and moves towards that person:

> Our generosity may leave us empty, but our emptiness then pulls gently at the whole until the thing in motion returns to replenish us. Social nature abhors a vacuum. Counsels Meister Eckhart, the mystic, 'Let us borrow empty vessels.' The gift finds that man attractive who stands with an empty bowl he does not own.[10]

Hyde declares, 'the gift does move from plenty to emptiness. It seeks the barren, the arid, the stuck, and the poor.'[11]

Art as gift

Hyde gives an account of the creative process by drawing on these insights about the gift economy. The process of the artist's labour begins with 'invocation' – that is, with the acceptance of the gift from beyond. The artist must accept her artistic talent, for instance, as a part of herself, but a part which she has not earned or deserved. And she must accept the inspiration that will lead to the production of particular works. Feeding her spirit will enable the artist to foster the conditions for such invocation to take place. Hyde quotes Meister Eckhart again, speaking of the need to create within ourselves the 'begging bowl' to which the gift of inspiration is drawn: 'It were a very grave defect in God if, finding thee so empty and so bare, he wrought no excellent work in thee nor primed thee with glorious gifts.'[12]

Once the gift has been received there is, of course, the labour of creativity in the transformation of this raw material. Artists hone their craft and their requisite skills, and work to manipulate the body of the work so that it is the best that it can be: on the page or the canvas, or in the music studio. However, Hyde is clear that the evaluation, clarification and revision involved in artistic activity are secondary tasks to that of invocation.

Once the gift has been accepted, and the labour is complete, the gift must be passed on. As the theory of gifts has it, the gift must keep moving. This explains the desire – felt imperative, even – that artists have to share their work with others: 'Publish or perish' is an internal demand of the creative spirit, and as long as the gift is passed on in this way, that same spirit will remain a stranger to the economics of scarcity. The perfection of one poem or painting does not render the writer or artist depleted and unable to continue to work. Rather, 'it is the talent which is not in use that is lost or atrophies, and to bestow one of our creations is the surest way to invoke the next'.[13]

Identity as gift

Central to this book is the conviction that the key to our identity is our uniqueness, and that this uniqueness is a divine gift. Having explored, with a great deal of help from Lewis Hyde, the nature of gifts and gifting and its role in human creativity, I would now like to draw out the implications for the ways in which we can live our identity as spiritual beings. My proposal, put simply, is that conceiving of ourselves and our identities as part of the economy of gift is what it means to be faithful.

To understand our identity as a gift, it helps to consider our lives as works of art, and ourselves as artists. We have seen already that we are each a story – or, more accurately, a complex collection of stories. Story-telling is an art. By story-telling I do not simply mean the verbal recounting of things that have happened to us and experiences that we have had (though that is usually part of the process). I mean taking the risk of sharing ourselves – in the broadest and deepest sense – with others; giving ourselves to others relationally, and opening ourselves up to their gift of themselves to us. If we think of our identity in this way, then telling our stories is about passing on the gift – keeping it in motion. This, in turn, as we have seen, will deepen the erotic bond and dissolve the boundaries both between ourselves and God (the originator of the gift), and between ourselves and others (those to whom we pass on the gift of ourselves, and from whom we receive).

Many of us are brought up with the notion that artists are special people with exceptional talents, but my suggestion is that each and every one of us is like an artist in that we have been given a gift. This is the gift of our singular life, though in passing on the gift we cease to be singular beings. As Hyde puts it:

The creative spirit moves in a body or ego larger than that of any single person. Works of art are drawn from, and their bestowal nourishes, those parts of our being that are not entirely personal, parts that derive from nature, from the group and the race, from history and tradition, and from the spiritual world.[14]

The lesson we learn from Hyde is that we are not individual masters of our own blank canvas, rustling up commodities to sell on to others. As he says, insofar as the artist is in receipt of a gift, there is an important sense in which the artist does not make the work. Rather, we are inheritors of that which is beyond our individual control, yet we are agents in a creative process whereby we work with what we have, and pass on the gift by sharing ourselves with others. In common with the schema of art as gift, so with identity we can conceive of three phases. Let's call these the 'phases of becoming': invocation, bestowal and growth. These phases interweave and overlap, for they are simultaneous processes.

1 Invocation

I have set before you life and death, blessings and curses. Choose life so that you and your descendants may live.'

Deuteronomy 30.19

To receive a gift, we have to be open to it. It may seem that the gift of life comes to us just once, at our birth, but this is not so. In biblical terms the gift of life is offered to us all the time, in many different ways, and if we are to be all that we can be, we need to learn how to embrace it. In order to become fully ourselves, we need to adopt the artist's attitude of invocation, creating within ourselves the begging bowl to which the gift of life is drawn. We need to feed our spirits so as to foster the conditions for invocation to take place. But how do we do this?

There is a clue to this in my meditation on the identity of Jesus. I describe him as having been, throughout his life, 'a process held open'; also as a passionate man, open and vulnerable to being affected by others. He was at various times rejected, hurt, despairing and abandoned. But he was also admired, desired, deferred to, and desperately and deeply loved. It would seem, therefore, that there is an important connection between being open, and being passionate.

In his autobiography Brian Thorne, person-centred counsellor and Christian theologian, writes movingly of the corruption of passionate desire that has taken hold in our world. Confusing desire with possessiveness, our society would have us believe that short-lived sexual obsession and its attendant destruction and doom are the inevitable outcomes of a passionate life. More often than not, Thorne suggests, this leads us to distrust our desiring and to cool our passion. He says,

> It would seem a risky undertaking in the circumstances to lead a life where it is possible to desire and to be desired, to be passionate and impassioned, to be free to convey and even to say, 'I love you' and yet not to fall into the cannibal's boiling cauldron where possessiveness, jealousy, envy, adultery, covetousness, selfishness, overwhelming pride and even murder constitute the rank ingredients.[15]

Yet he keeps faith with the notion that we can dare to be fully alive – that we may trust in a form of loving where we wish neither to possess the other nor to be possessed; thereby allowing ourselves to be fully present to one another, with all our desiring and yearning. And he stubbornly resists the gloomy analysis of our perversely sexualized culture that, he admits, has 'sapped my energy and condemned me for a while to a kind of half-life where I have forgotten or no longer believed that the glory of God is reflected in men and women fully alive'.[16]

Being a 'process held open', then, enables us to be men and women 'fully alive'. This, in turn, is exactly the gift Jesus claimed he had come to bring – life in all its fullness. But embracing the possibilities of this involves, as Thorne points out, a life of resistance to the many forces around us that would have us settle for less. So what is it that we are embracing, and what is involved in this life of resistance?

Therapist Carl Rogers claims that

> Life, at its best, is a flowing, changing process in which nothing is fixed. In my clients and in myself I find that when life is richest and most rewarding it is a flowing process. To experience this is both fascinating and a little frightening. I find I am at my best when I can let the flow of my experience carry me, in a direction which appears to be forward, toward goals of which I am but dimly aware. In thus floating with the complex stream of my experiencing, and in trying to understand the ever-changing complexity, it should be evident that there are no fixed points. When I am thus able to be in process, it is clear that there can be no closed system of beliefs, no unchanging set of principles which I hold. Life is guided by a changing understanding of and interpretation of my experience. It is always in a process of becoming.[17]

Rogers' description of life at its best is characterized by movement. Not surprising, perhaps, given that the economy of gift is all about momentum. Being in process, in Rogers' terms, or being a process held open, is a way of invoking, in an ongoing way, the gift of life within us. And it is this gift that enables us to be fully alive and wholly ourselves. Identity, then, is a fluid and constantly changing process that we embrace, rather than a static acquisition that we possess.

There is another image that might help us here. In his exploration of art as gift, Hyde engages at some depth with the poet Walt Whitman, and one particular work entitled 'Song of Myself'. As the title suggests, this is a meditation on self and identity. As part of this, Whitman delights at the passage of 'stuff' through his body: 'My respiration and inspiration, the beating of my heart, the passing of blood and air through my lungs.' Hyde suggests that

The 'self' that Whitman's song presents to us is a sort of lung, inhaling and exhaling the world. Almost everything in the poem happens as a breathing, an incarnate give-and-take, which filters the world through the body. Whitman says of a long list of people and occupations, 'these tend inward to me, and I tend outward to them . . . /And of these . . . I weave the song of myself . . . ' Whitman speaks of his inhalation as 'accepting' the bounty of the world, his exhalation as 'bequeathing' or 'bestowing' (himself, his work).[18]

Crucial to Whitman is the notion that breathing involves both inhaling and exhaling: taking in (receiving), and giving out (passing on the gift). He sums up the imperative of this two-way process most poignantly when he says,

> Dazzling and tremendous how quick the sunrise would
> kill me,
> If I could not now and always send sunrise out of me.[19]

In summary, then, we might say that invocation involves faith in, and cultivation of, a sense of ourselves as permeable, in flow, changing. Insofar as it can ever be fixed, our identity is located in that pause between inhaling and exhaling – between receiving giftedness from God, the world and others, and passing it on: exhaling, bestowing, creating.

2 Bestowal

Jesus understood his own identity in terms of the bestowal of a gift. He talked of himself in terms of food and drink that must be consumed – he said he was 'the bread of life' and 'the living bread that came down from heaven'. He was always feeding people, sometimes in their thousands, and he broke the Sabbath rules to assuage hunger, angry that religion was getting in the way of a free-flowing gift. Jesus gave his own body and blood to his friends to eat and drink in the symbolic form of bread and wine at the Last Supper, saying, 'Whoever eats me will live because of me.' And he gave his life in real terms on the cross. The purpose of that gift was erotic – that is, to restore connection; to dissolve the boundary between the divine and the human.

In the teachings of Jesus we see how to live with our giftedness; to be all that we can be. Jesus addressed, again and again, the temptation that all humanity faces to hold on to what has been given to us, to stop the gift in its tracks. It seems prudent to us to protect what we have become – to nurse our achievements without taking further risks; to opt for the small, the safe, the secure, both in terms of relationships and identity. In telling his own story, however, Jesus showed us how to keep the gift in motion. He made it clear that unless we do this, the gift will die. As he put it, 'Whoever would save his life will lose it, and whoever loses his life for my sake will find it. For what does it profit a man, if he gains the whole world and forfeits his life?' Looked at in this light, a whole clutch of Jesus' sayings make new sense. He said, 'Love one another as I have loved you,' for what else can one do with the gift of love but pass it on? In the same vein he declared, 'Freely you have received, now freely give.' And in the economy of gift, it is obvious that the treasure that is buried in a field will come out less valuable than when it went in; yeast is useless if it is not dispersed in dough; and the seed that does not die will not multiply a hundredfold. Only in bestowal and dissolution is there growth.

3 Growth

Enlarge the place of your tent, and let the curtains of your habitations be stretched out; hold not back, lengthen your cords and strengthen your stakes. For you will spread abroad to the right and to the left, and your descendants will possess the nations and will people the desolate cities.

Isaiah 54.2–4

Isaiah Chapter 54 is the story of a barren woman, and I want to explore it here because it represents a splendid rendition of how gifts work. The imagery is of one who has been cruelly oppressed for a lifetime. To be childless in the ancient world was, as we know, deeply shameful. To be barren was to be a loser, a failure, marginalized and worthless. In terms of the circulation of gifts, therefore, this woman is the 'empty place' – she is the one who has been without for the longest time. She is desperate for liberation. And so it comes. The momentum of the gift gravitates towards her. First, she is exhorted to behave as though her freedom were already a reality, to 'Sing, O barren one, who did not bear; break forth into singing and cry aloud' (verse 1). By some mysterious process, this singing invokes the gift, and the process of her liberation begins. Significantly, in this process the receiving of a gift is indistinguishable from passing it on – bestowing it on others. She is invited to 'Enlarge' her tent (verses 2–4). The promise is that this enlargement will set in train a process of growth that, in the end, will result in her descendants possessing the nations and peopling desolate cities. The language used to describe what is coming her way is that of excess and extravagance. Her foundations are to be laid with sapphires, her pinnacles will be made of agate, and her walls will be of precious stones (verses 11–13). Oppression, terror and strife will be far away.

Shame, perhaps more than any other human emotion, leads to self-protection. The humiliation of it leaves us with a desire to hold on to what little sense of ourselves remains. The message of this story (a symbol which stands for so much more, of course) is that it is in letting go and extending herself that liberation comes to the barren woman. It is in being 'stretched out', not in holding back, that the gift does its work. She is called to expansion, not to contraction.

The paradox of identity is that holding on to who we are leads to contraction. If we try to grasp our identity too tightly to ourselves; if we try to maintain it in a static state as a stable foundation, we stop the gift, and so a part of us dies or loses its vitality.

Whether this be our faith identity, our sexual identity, our way of analysing the world, or our status as dominator or dominated, this paradox holds true. If it becomes fixed, our identity can become an empty category – a prison that stops us from living with nuance and change. In the spirit of Isaiah, at the moment when we begin to feel safe and secure, and that we know who we are and who are 'our people', it is perhaps wise to keep a weather-eye on the boundaries of our tent, and whether it might be made bigger lest it begin to shrink.

My concluding reflection, therefore, is that identity is like floating, or like Walt Whitman's breathing. This is not an atomized floating where we are free from connection, with no strings attached. On the contrary, it is a form of passionate commitment: to embracing the gift of our singularity, while allowing that singularity to dissolve and give way to something greater. And in turn, that something greater will give new meaning to our singularity. And so it goes on – the constant circulation of the gift of our identity, connecting us ever more closely with one another and with God.

Notes

1 Questions of identity

1 Sebastian Moore, *Let This Mind Be In You: The Quest for Identity through Oedipus to Christ* (London: DLT, 1985), p. 23. Reproduced by kind permission.

2 Moore, *Let This Mind Be In You*, p. 25.

3 Donna J. Haraway, *Simians, Cyborgs, and Women: The Reinvention of Nature* (London: Free Association Books, 1991), p. 206.

4 Carl R. Rogers, *On Becoming a Person: A Therapist's View of Psychotherapy* (London: Constable, 2004; 1st edn 1967), p. 26.

5 John Gray, *Men Are From Mars, Women Are From Venus* (New York: HarperCollins, 1992).

2 Others

1 B. C. Hutchens, *Levinas: A Guide for the Perplexed* (London and New York: Continuum, 2004), p. 19.

2 From transcribed notes of a lecture entitled 'The Challenge of the Other: Towards Dialogic Psychotherapy and Counselling', by Peter F. Schmid, Sigmund Freud University, Vienna Institute for Person-Centred Studies, Austria. Lecture given on 18 May 2006 at the University of Strathclyde Counselling Unit at a conference entitled 'Meeting at Relational Depth: A One Day Conference Celebrating the Work of Dave Mearns'.

3 Schmid, 'The Challenge of the Other'.

4 Sebastian Moore, *Let This Mind Be In You: The Quest for Identity through Oedipus to Christ* (London: DLT, 1985), p. 17.

5 Moore, *Let This Mind Be In You*, p. 17.

6 Moore, *Let This Mind Be In You*, p. 18.

7 Moore, *Let This Mind Be In You*, p. 19.

8 Moore, *Let This Mind Be In You*, p. 19.

9 Moore, *Let This Mind Be In You*, p. 19.

10 Moore, *Let This Mind Be In You*, p. 23.

3 Power

1 Susan Engel, *Context is Everything: The Nature of Memory* (New York: Freeman, 2000), pp. 40–1.
2 Engel, *Context is Everything*, p. 41.
3 Engel, *Context is Everything*, p. 5.
4 Engel, *Context is Everything*, p. 6.
5 Engel, *Context is Everything*, p. 36.
6 Engel, *Context is Everything*, p. 44.
7 Engel, *Context is Everything*, p. 41.
8 Engel, *Context is Everything*, p. 87.
9 Quoted by Ann Memmott in 'Welcoming Those with Autism and Asperger's Syndrome' (Oxford Diocesan Board for Social Responsibility, 2008).
10 Personal email correspondence, reproduced with permission.
11 Richard Dyer, *White* (London and New York: Routledge, 1997), p. xiv.
12 Dyer, *White*, p. xiv.
13 Dyer, *White*, p. 1.
14 Dyer, *White*, pp. 1–2.
15 Maureen Walker and Jean Baker Miller, 'Racial Images and Relational Possibilities', in Judith V. Jordan, Maureen Walker and Linda M. Hartling (eds), *The Complexity of Connection: Writings from the Stone Center's Jean Baker Miller Training Institute* (New York: The Guilford Press, 2004), pp. 130–1. Reproduced by permission of The Guilford Press.
16 Walker and Miller, 'Racial Images and Relational Possibilities', p. 141.
17 Robert Jensen, *The Heart of Whiteness: Confronting Race, Racism and White Privilege* (San Francisco: City Lights, 2005), p. 25.
18 Dyer, *White*, p. 10.
19 Jackie Stacey, *Teratologies: A Cultural Study of Cancer* (London: Routledge, 1997), p. 5. Reproduced by kind permission.
20 Stacey, *Teratologies*, pp. 8–9.
21 Stacey, *Teratologies*, p. 9.
22 Stacey, *Teratologies*, pp. 14–15.
23 Stacey, *Teratologies*, p. 21.
24 Dave Mearns and Mick Cooper, *Working at Relational Depth in Counselling and Psychotherapy* (London: Sage, 2005), p. 4.
25 Mearns and Cooper, *Working at Relational Depth in Counselling and Psychotherapy*, p. 5.
26 Jordan, Walker and Hartling (eds), *The Complexity of Connection*, p. 2.
27 Jordan, Walker and Hartling (eds), *The Complexity of Connection*, pp. 4–5.
28 Stacey, *Teratologies*, p. 65.
29 Stacey, *Teratologies*, p. 66.
30 Stacey, *Teratologies*, pp. 69–70.
31 bell hooks, *Talking Back: Thinking Feminist, Thinking Black* (Boston, MA: South End Press, 1989), p. 12.

4 Faith

1 'Drudgery or Freedom' was published as one of my regular columns in the *Door* newspaper, Diocese of Oxford, July 2007.

2 These responses appeared on the website of the Diocese of Oxford, <www.oxford.anglican.org>.

3 Carl Rogers, *A Way of Being* (New York: Mariner Books, 1995), p. 10. Excerpts from A WAY OF BEING by Carl Rogers. Copyright © 1980 by Houghton Mifflin Company. Reprinted by permission of Houghton Mifflin Harcourt Publishing Company. All rights reserved.

4 Rogers, *A Way of Being*, p. 22.

5 Sebastian Moore, *Let This Mind Be In You: The Quest for Identity through Oedipus to Christ* (London: DLT, 1985), p. 17.

5 Extending ourselves

1 From Lewis Hyde, *The Gift: How the Creative Spirit Transforms the World* (Edinburgh: Canongate, 2006), p. xiv. First published in Great Britain by Canongate Books Ltd, 14 High Street, Edinburgh, EH1 1TE. Reproduced by kind permission.

2 Hyde, *The Gift*, p. xiv.

3 Hyde, *The Gift*, p. xiv.

4 Hyde, *The Gift*, pp. xiv–xv.

5 Hyde, *The Gift*, p. 4.

6 Hyde, *The Gift*, p. 5.

7 Hyde, *The Gift*, p. 9.

8 Hyde, *The Gift*, p. 63.

9 Hyde, *The Gift*, p. 22.

10 Hyde, *The Gift*, p. 24.

11 Hyde, *The Gift*, p. 25.

12 Hyde, *The Gift*, p. 146.

13 Hyde, *The Gift*, p. 148.

14 Hyde, *The Gift*, p. 155.

15 Brian Thorne, *Love's Embrace: The Autobiography of a Person-Centred Therapist* (Ross-on-Wye: PCCS Books, 2005), p. 218.

16 Thorne, *Love's Embrace*, p. 218.

17 Carl R. Rogers, *On Becoming a Person: A Therapist's View of Psychotherapy* (London: Constable, 2004; 1st edn 1967), p. 27.

18 Hyde, *The Gift*, p. 174.

19 Hyde, *The Gift*, p. 174.

Suggested further reading

Bauman, Zygmunt, *Identity* (London: Polity, 2004).

Bryden, Christine, *Dancing with Dementia: My Story of Living Positively with Dementia* (London and Philadelphia: Jessica Kingsley, 2005).

Dyer, Richard, *White* (London and New York: Routledge, 1997).

Engel, Susan, *Context is Everything: The Nature of Memory* (New York: Freeman, 2000).

Greenfield, Susan, *ID: The Quest for Identity in the 21st Century* (London: Sceptre, 2008).

Hemmings, Clare, *Bisexual Spaces: A Geography of Sexuality and Gender* (New York and London: Routledge, 2002).

Hutchens, B. C., *Levinas: A Guide for the Perplexed* (London and New York: Continuum, 2004).

Hyde, Lewis, *The Gift: How the Creative Spirit Transforms the World* (Edinburgh: Canongate, 2006).

Jensen, Robert, *The Heart of Whiteness: Confronting Race, Racism and White Privilege* (San Francisco: City Lights, 2005).

Jordan, Judith V., Walker, Maureen and Hartling, Linda M. (eds), *The Complexity of Connection: Writings from the Stone Center's Jean Baker Miller Training Institute* (New York: The Guilford Press, 2004).

Mearns, Dave and Cooper, Mick, *Working at Relational Depth in Counselling and Psychotherapy* (London: Sage, 2005).

Moore, Sebastian, *Let This Mind Be In You: The Quest for Identity through Oedipus to Christ* (London: DLT, 1985).

Neuberger, Julia, *Not Dead Yet: A Manifesto for Old Age* (London: Harper-Collins, 2008).

Robbins, Jill (ed.), *Is it Righteous to Be? Interviews with Emmanuel Levinas* (Stanford, CA: Stanford University Press, 2001).

Rogers, Carl R., *On Becoming a Person: A Therapist's View of Psychotherapy* (London: Constable, 2004; 1st edn 1967).

Rogers, Carl, *A Way of Being* (New York: Mariner Books, 1995).

Stacey, Jackie, *Teratologies: A Cultural Study of Cancer* (London: Routledge, 1997).

Thorne, Brian, *Love's Embrace: The Autobiography of a Person-Centred Therapist* (Ross-on-Wye: PCCS Books, 2005).

Thorne, Brian, *Person-centred Counselling and Christian Spirituality: The Secular and the Holy* (London: Whurr, 2000).

Vincent, Norah, *Self Made Man: My Year Disguised as a Man* (London: Atlantic Books, 2006).

Ware, Vron and Back, Les, *Out of Whiteness: Color, Politics and Culture* (Chicago and London: University of Chicago Press, 2002).

Webster, Alison, *Found Wanting: Women, Christianity and Sexuality* (London: Cassell, 1995).

Webster, Alison, *Wellbeing* (London: SCM Press, 2002).